In *The Gulf Between Us* Iraqi, American, Palestinian, Egyptian, Jordanian and British women and men – writers, military analysts, doctors, academics, journalists – explore the dynamics, the politics and the tragedies of the Gulf War.

**Victoria Brittain** is a journalist and writer, author of *Hidden Lives, Hidden Deaths*, a book about Southern Africa. She worked in Vietnam, and then in Africa for ten years, and has been editor of the *Guardian*'s Third World Review. She is currently Assistant Foreign Editor at the *Guardian*.

# THE GULF
# BETWEEN US

## The Gulf War and Beyond

*Edited by Victoria Brittain*

Published by VIRAGO PRESS Limited 1991
20–23 Mandela Street, Camden Town, London NW1 0HQ

A CIP catalogue record for this title
is available from the British Library

Typeset by CentraCet, Cambridge

Printed and bound in Great Britain by
Cox & Wyman Ltd, Reading, Berkshire

# CONTENTS

Acknowledgements vii

Map of the Middle East viii

Introduction *Victoria Brittain* ix

The Unnecessary War *Alexander Cockburn and Andrew Cohen* 1

Roots of An Adventure
The Invasion of Kuwait: Iraqi Political Dynamics
*Faleh' Abd al Jabar* 27

Victory in the Desert: Superior Technology or Brute Force?
*Rear Admiral Gene R. La Rocque and
Rear Admiral Eugene J. Carroll, Jr* 43

Something about the Peace Movement:
Something about the People's Right *Not* to Know
*Grace Paley* 61

Tales of War: Arab Women in the Eye of the Storm
*Dr Fadia Faqir* 77

Egypt's Central Role *Haifaa Khalafallah* 89

War-Guilt, Zinoviev and the Boring Canadian *Edward Pearce* 97

The NHS and its Patients: Casualities of the Gulf War
*Dr Lesley Morrison* 107

The Deepening Tragedy of the Palestinians *Abbas Shiblak* 119

Poisoned Sand and Seas *John Vidal* 133

Wanted: A New Policy for the United Nations *Barbara Rogers* 143

Epilogue: Making Sense of an Earthquake *Roger Owen* 159

Autobiography Poem *Sadiq al Saygh* 179

Notes on Contributors 183

# ACKNOWLEDGEMENTS

Many people helped to produce this book at great speed. I want to thank all the authors for their readiness to put other things aside to meet short deadlines, and for the generous help with discussions on early drafts which several of them gave me too.

I also want to thank Jan Parker, Melanie McFadyean, Thea Sharrock, Cas Knight, Richard McKerrow and John Gittings for practical help in many different ways, and Lennie Goodings, our editor at Virago, for her enthusiastic support and limitless patience.

In addition, I am very grateful to Noam Chomsky, Richard Falk and Albert Hourani for critical interventions in the genesis of the book.

*Victoria Brittain*
*London, April 1991*

# INTRODUCTION

*Victoria Brittain*

Bulldozers scooped the uncounted bodies of Iraqi soldiers from the collapsed trenches of Kuwait and Southern Iraq into shallow mass graves far from the eyes of reporters, and with a hasty violation of the First Geneva Convention.[1] No one knows if these young men and boys, who may have been buried alive in their trenches during the Allies' six-week air bombardment, or may have starved to death, or may have been shot from helicopters or crushed by B-52s as they retreated in the hundred-hour ground war, numbered 50,000, or 100,000 as the Americans say, or 150,000, or 200,000 as some Israeli sources put it. Gradually some figures will leak out as months pass without sons or husbands returning home and families lose hope, but who will bother to count the missing? Neither the Allies nor the regime of Saddam Hussein have any interest in these unknown people.

An instant book is a poor memorial to them and historians will write more powerful ones, but this one grew out of the conviction that their traumatic experience must quickly be brought into the lives of Westerners who understood it so little that they gave overwhelming support in the polls to the leaders of the US-led coalition which carried out an illegal war by immoral means. The gulf between us, from the allied countries, and those who have suffered so unimaginably in Iraq and its diaspora, is unbridgeable. One historian has written here, with the long perspective of his profession, an indictment of this, the most destructive Western involvement in the region. But it is the Arab writers in this collection, particularly the two Iraqis with long years of exile, whose voices best convey the depth of the tragedy which George Bush and Saddam Hussein brought to their people.

The vast majority of the men who died never fought and were not even soldiers in any normal use of the word, but students, peasants, teachers, civil servants, taxi drivers, rounded up by the Ba'ath Party machine as cannon fodder for the front line in Kuwait.

After Saddam Hussein ordered their withdrawal from Kuwait, Iraqi vehicles flying white flags were backed up for miles with planes dropping anti-personnel bombs on them before finishing off with B-52s. They were massacred 'like shooting fish in a barrel', as one US pilot put it. He described the carrier ship *Ranger* with the *William Tell* overture blasting from every speaker on every deck as crews frantically reloaded planes for another swipe at the roads north of Kuwait City.[2] Some pilots' descriptions of the terrified faces of the 'sheep shoot' they caught in their lights as men ran wildly in a hopeless attempt to escape inevitable death, like those in the unbroken wall of wrecked and firebombed vehicles blocked retreating on the highway at Al Mutlaa, are the images of the Gulf war which never stuck in public consciousness because they were never filmed. In this war, instant history was made by television.

Nor is there any official estimate of the equally invisible civilian casualties from the day-and-night Allied bombing of towns, villages, roads and bridges hundreds of miles from Kuwait which reduced Iraqi lives to a primitive struggle for survival on minimal food rations and without electricity, water, sewerage, communications or fuel. The capital, Baghdad, wrote Richard Reid of UNICEF, was like a body 'with its skin basically intact, with every main bone broken and with its joints and tendons cut'.

Nor can anyone guess at the much greater toll of deaths, maiming, trauma and terror of the civil war which gripped the south and much of the north and east of Iraq as various Kurdish parties, Communists, Islamic, Shiite parties, angry retreating soldiers including even Takriti senior officers, and Arab soldiers defecting to the uprising in the north, fought the Republican Guard and other army units in the anarchy which followed the Iraqi government's capitulation to the Allied ground war.

As control of major cities from the mountainous north to the desert south veered from one side to the other, and whole units changed sides in despair and confusion, uncounted heaps of corpses lay in the streets to be eaten by dogs, or swung from Republican Guard tank turrets to terrorize those who had dared, for a few days, to deface the omnipresent symbol of Ba'ath power – portraits of Saddam Hussein. The vengeance of the victors on the defenceless hundreds of thousands attempting to flee the country through the northern mountains recalled not only Saddam Hussein's earlier attempts to reduce the Kurdish population drastically, such as the chemical attack on Halabja in 1988, but the clear US policy to decimate Iraq's million-man army.

The first outsiders into Iraq after the Allied war, on a series of UN missions, described the situation as catastrophic, with famine and epidemics threatening fresh waves of death. American soldiers in the no-man's-land they occupied north of Kuwait's frontier were horrified at the scenes of human misery as abandoned children begged for food, Iraqi soldiers pleaded to desert, some then had to be separated from enraged civilian refugees – and meanwhile military doctors struggled to save the lives of women and children with wounds putrefying after days without treatment. Across Kurdistan, in the first days of the doomed uprising, towns rebelled against the Ba'ath regime and were backed by Peshmerga partisan units. With the exception of Kirkuk there was no fight, and Arab soldiers in their thousands set out to walk away from a civil war they never wanted to engage in, towards homes and families perhaps destroyed beyond recovery. Within days Kurds were fleeing in their hundreds of thousands in the opposite direction, seeking refuge in Iran or Turkey from an onslaught from the Iraqi government loyalists.

All this untallied human suffering of Iraqis was, so the Allies said, to restore to Kuwait its sovereignty, and the feudal government of the Al Sabah family which ruled it before the illegal seizure of the country by Iraq on 2 August 1990. The often-repeated assertions of President Bush, the British ambassador at the United Nations, Sir Davd Hannay, and others that the Allies had no wish to penalize the population of Iraq but only the country's ruler, rang hollow when every day of war brought a devastation so complete that the UN missions said it would be years before even an emergency programme could bring the country back from what Marti Ahtisaari's UN report called the pre-industrial state the bombing reduced it to. Others described an Iraq returned to the Stone Age.

No talk of a UN mandate, or of a just war, can ever make the destruction of Iraq anything but a shameful stain on the conscience of the Allies rather than the victory of Operation Desert Storm hailed by the Allied leadership and an overwhelmingly triumphalist Western media. It is a further shame that there has been no challenge to the hypocrisy of the changing war aims of the Allies, who wanted not just Kuwait, with all its oil wealth, back under control of a pro-Western government, not only the ousting of Saddam Hussain, but also a new regime in Baghdad which would be destabilized neither by Shiites demanding an 'Islamic republic', nor by a democratic movement looking for genuine popular partici-pation and Kurdish autonomy. In the weeks following the end of the Allied fighting, the vacuum of strategy from Washington became ever more obvious, and the Kurdish people have been its most tragic victims. To cover the vacuum, in an extraordinary collective delusion, the Allies chose to deny their responsibility, with Saddam Hussein, for genocide too terrible for Western public opinion to swallow.

The unquantifiable suffering of the Iraqi people in the war and the anarchy which followed came after long years of uncounted costs of a dictatorship which murdered tens of thousands of its citizens and broke, corrupted or forced into exile a generation of its finest writers and thinkers. From a population of 17 million one-tenth were in exile even before the turmoil of 1991. Alexander Cockburn and Andrew Cohen detail the deep complicity of succes-sive US administrations with this tyranny. Throughout these different phases of recent Iraqi history the interests of the Ba'athist regime of President Saddam Hussein and those of the Allies – the

USA, Britain, France, Germany and the Soviet Union – who first supported him, mainly with arms sales, and then set out to destroy him, coincided in the masking of these realities. T. S. Eliot's 'human kind cannot bear very much reality' could have been written for the Iraq no one outside wanted to know.

For years Iraq, the cradle of one of the oldest civilizations in the world, home of poets and philosophers revered in the Arab region, had been transformed by Saddam Hussein's dictatorship. The exiled poet Sadiq al Saygh writes of the harsh choice all Iraqi intellectuals faced: of becoming a state intellectual, with all the privileges and comfort that offers, or writing the truth and facing 'death in a muddy ditch' (which could also describe exile for many). Loss of home and family, of profession, of identity, are the common pain of exile, but for Iraqis all that was compounded by the ever-present terror of death from the security services.

In 1988 the pseudonymous Iraqi writer in exile Samir al-Khalil described what he called a new Third World style of barbarism:

> a society that used to revel in politics is not only subdued and silent, but profoundly apolitical. Fear is the agency of that transformation; the kind of fear that comes not only from what the neighbours might say, but that makes people careful of what they say in front of their children . . . this new kind of fear drove through all private space.

Prophetically, he wrote: 'The hidden potential for even more violence inside Iraq could at some point in the future make the Lebanese civil war look like a family outing gone slightly sour.'[3]

In the years when people like Samir al-Khalil were being driven into exile, it was not just the West and the Soviet Union which were determined not to see what was happening in Iraq. This tragic and deformed society was to have succeeded Cuba as the leader of the Non-Aligned Movement, and preparations to host the Non-Aligned Summit in 1982 were well advanced in Baghdad. Only the Iran–Iraq War, launched by Saddam Hussein three years earlier, got the Summit postponed on security grounds and moved to New Delhi, depriving the President of the crown of Third World leadership which would have bestowed on him in many eyes the heroic status of Gamal Abdel Nasser.

In fact that mantle was still put upon him during the Gulf War by millions of people for whom his defiance of the unpopular rich Arab states of the Gulf, of Western, and particularly American power, was enough to wipe out criticism for the seizure of Kuwait. For the hundreds of thousands who demonstrated for him, or bought his portrait in street markets from Delhi and Jakarta to Amman, Algiers, Rabat and Lagos, Saddam Hussein became the symbol of a poor man's pride, and of the Third World standing up against the technology and arrogance of a United States bent on extending control over the region's oil wealth. In another collective delusion, many of these people actually believed that Iraq – a small Third World country with a huge expenditure on arms but an undistinguished record in the long war with Iran, despite significant aid from the USA – would win the war against the most powerful countries in the world. That illusion, exploded in the first hours of the war, tells much about the level of desperation in these societies – a desperation so deep that it will seize on any source of pride, any identification with a power that could promise a psychological release from the pain of poverty and increasing marginalization in an alien technological world.

Many Iraqi and other Arab intellectuals who knew better what the trial of strength would do to Iraq and the region, and who knew too the terrible price Saddam Hussein's regime had exacted from the country, spoke eloquently against the Allies' war project as it gathered ominous weight through the autumn of 1990. Another exiled Iraqi writer, Faleh' Abd al Jabar, who writes on the internal impetus towards the invasion of Kuwait, warned in the *Guardian* in the early days of the war that the Allies' choice of war, rather than the slow grind of sanctions coupled with political negotiations, would destroy the country, but give Saddam Hussein another political lease of life. The military, he wrote, was the main force in the country which could remove Saddam Hussein and offer a chance of change in Iraq, but they could not do so while fighting an external enemy. In Washington though, the policy-makers stopped short of understanding how the war was blocking that change. More than a month after the end of the war, specialists in the Defense Department began belatedly to come to the same conclusion as the revolts spread across the country. 'No military is going to overthrow Saddam Hussein while they are fighting a rebellion,' said Phebe Marr of the National Defense University, admitting then that the fighting was strengthening, not weakening, Saddam Hussein.

The Americans, obsessed with Eastern European parallels and expecting a Ceausescu-style end for Saddam Hussein, chose not to listen to the voices from the region which told them this and many other awkward truths about the war's probable consequences. Many Arab writers foresaw the terrible human costs throughout the region and for the hundreds of thousands of Asian guest workers, the unprecedented environmental catastrophe – which John Vidal describes – and the destabilization of the region's power balance which would leave Israel as an unchallengeable force further than ever from giving the Palestinians their homeland. Abbas Shiblak describes how that long, festering injustice has been compounded by the war.

The new postwar order in the region, announced a month after the war as to be run from an American command centre in Bahrain, policed with Egyptian and Syrian soldiers, and paid for by the rich Gulf States, was the realization of an American policy goal sought by successive US administrations since the overthrow of their long-time regional ally, the Shah of Iran, in 1979. For many Arabs such a tangible reinforcement of American military power in the region – a considerable escalation from the familiar naval presence – was a humiliating return to colonial power relations, carrying the seeds of an inevitable destabilization to the regimes which might initially welcome it.

For the USA this war – or a variant of it which would inevitably take place in the unstable Middle East, with control over oil as the trigger – was one Washington had been preparing for even as the arms trade with Iraq flourished in the late 1980s. In 1988 the US Commission on Integrated Long-term Strategy underlined the new threat to the USA of strong regional powers with large, well-equipped armies. As any threat from the Soviet Union disappeared with the end of the Cold War, in the early months of the Bush Administration, Middle Intensity Conflict became the preoccupation of the planners. The US military began to prepare itself to face conflicts with what President Bush himself called 'renegade regimes' in the Third World. Spelt out by Defense Secretary Richard Cheney in secret planning documents for the period 1992–7, Middle Intensity Conflict was clearly targeting Iraq and Syria.[4]

Post-Vietnam, with American military confidence at its lowest ebb, the Pentagon's fashion was for Low Intensity Conflicts (LICs) where no US casualties would come home to haunt the politicians. In the 1980s, under LIC, US proxies destroyed the new nationalist governments of small, weak Third World countries such as Nicaragua and Angola, working for transformation of extremely backward nations by social justice. They openly aspired to socialism, and in both the achievements in education and health were an example to their two regions much praised ten years ago by international agencies, but now battered beyond recognition after a decade or more of terrorism funded and encouraged by the USA. Iraq too, even under the dictatorship, had built an impressive education and health service, improved transport and supplied villages with electricity in a sweep of nationalist development which was a casualty of the Allied precision bombing which took out sewage treatment plants, electricity generators, and all communications links. As under Low Intensity Conflict, the first victims of Middle Intensity Conflict were civilians.

Perhaps never has there been a war in which the contrast between the image and the actual events has been so acute. Becoming a propaganda machine for the Pentagon and the weapons manufacturers, the media mostly showed a war without bodies, a war without suffering, a war that was a wonder of technology. Rear

Admirals Gene La Rocque and Eugene J. Carroll, Jr describe in detail the military picture we never saw.

Cable News Network, whose journalists came close to being actors, not reporters, with its illusion of covering every aspect of the war, actually made it almost impossible to understand. In a wonderful gesture of revolt against the illusion that the viewers were getting information, described in an article entitled 'Did you say Liberation?', the Moroccan writer Driss Chraibi threw his television out of the window of his third-floor flat in Paris as the jubilant announcer described the first 'smart' bombs falling on Iraq. The saturation television coverage – epitomized by the repetition of the film clips which showed a 'smart' bomb hitting its precise target and coasting down a chimney – deliberately obscured the fact that only 7 per cent of the explosives dropped were 'smart' bombs which were indeed 90 per cent accurate. By the time the US air force revealed that 70 per cent of the 88,500 tons of explosives dropped over Iraq and Kuwait in forty-three days of war missed their targets, it was too late to change the image of technological success imprinted by television. And with this image that war is an easy business for Americans and those who choose to ally with them, an unmistakable ideological message about global power relations went out.

The short war has laid the ghost of the much-vaunted independence of the Western media. From the commentator who gave us the description of the bombs falling on Baghdad as 'the Fourth of July party', to those who used the military jargon of 'surgical strikes', 'theatre of operations' and 'collateral damage' when they meant civilian deaths and injuries, there was the same use of misleading words to distance the reader or viewer from the effects of the war. The extraordinary spinelessness of most of the media – accepting without challenge unprecedented measures of government control in both the USA and Britain – is the subject of Edward Pearce's chapter. The pool reporters controlled in Saudi Arabia and Bahrain by the Ministry of Defence sent back unmemorable censored copy. Journalists who chose not to join the pool were sharply criticized not only by the authorities, but even by other journalists. Some, most notably Robert Fisk writing in the *Independent*, did manage to do a reporter's job with distinction. However, it was Paul Foot and John Pilger, based in London, who by their writing and broadcasting, and by starting the 600-strong anti-censorship, anti-war campaign of Media Workers Against the War, saved our profession from becoming His Master's Voice.

Retired military officers, with a very different style from the two writing in this book, became the staple diet of television, radio and newspaper columns. They set a tone of unquestioning support for the means used to fulfil the official Allied war aims as they shifted from those expressed in August as the defence of Saudi Arabia and the restoration of the government of Kuwait, to the crushing of the Iraqi military machine and the country's industrial potential, to the removal of Saddam Hussein himself, which had gradually become accepted by the start of the war in January. The unspoken decision to escalate from a limited war over Kuwait to the bombing campaign of Iraq itself is in sharp contrast to the choice of limited wars made, for instance, by the French in Algeria, or even the USA in Vietnam.

The media were not alone in equating unquestioning support for the war with patriotism. With a few honourable exceptions – led in Britain by Tony Benn – the British Labour Party, trade unions and churches, the American Democrats, and the French Socialist Party were part of the sad capitulation to the monolithic support demanded, and received, by the US government. An autonomous European political line disappeared overnight. The transformation of the French position from President Mitterrand's September speech at the United Nations, which highlighted the hopes of negotiations, to January's unconditional support for the USA, with the jettisoning of France's traditional special ties with many in the Arab world – all without a debate – is more striking that the predictable British following of the US line.

Within the United Nations itself, as Barbara Rogers writes, the dominance of the Americans, displayed in the early days as a diplomacy which benefited from the new post-Cold War international unity, turned the negotiations on a cease-fire into unprecedented political controls over the defeated enemy. Earlier ideas for an international conference to tackle the region's fundamental problems – including, as well as the Palestinians' future, the question of arms control and the possession of nuclear weapons by Israel and the chemical and biological arsenal of Iraq – disappeared from the international agenda in favour of an American resolution of unprecedented severity which would penalize Iraq economically as well as militarily for decades, and give the Security Council the right to guarantee its frontiers.

In all these Allied countries the echoes of the totalitarian days of McCarthyism in the United States, even of the attitudes of 1930s European Fascism, were evoked by the response to the few great intellectuals who denounced the war – Günter Grass, John Berger, Claude Julien, Régis Debray, Noam Chomsky, Robert J. Lifton, Richard Falk – and to the many anonymous people who massed in anti-war rallies in Europe and the United States. Their views, as Grace Paley writes, virtually disappeared. Fashionable intellectuals in Europe derided the anti-war movement as a shallow anti-Americanism. President Bush, with the unprecedented approval rating of 91 per cent of Americans behind him, was unchallenged in the duplicity and arrogance which allowed him on 15 February 1991 to call on the Iraqi people to remove Saddam Hussein and the next month to get away with the staggering statement that there could be no interference by the USA in Iraq's internal affairs. The CIA had, though, been authorized by the President in January to aid Saudi-supported rebel factions, according to several intelligence sources, and NBC News in the USA reported that The Voice of Free Iraq, a clandestine radio station operating during the Gulf crisis, was CIA-sponsored.[5]

The 91 per cent approval rating speaks loud on what Professor Noam Chomsky has called the 'manufactured consent' of American democracy. The same phenomenon explains the long and profound disinterest in Washington or London in the lack of democracy in Iraq, or elsewhere in the Middle East, which would have prevented first the rise of Saddam Hussein's dictatorship, second the provocative follies of the Kuwaiti oligarchy, and third the cover of Saudi, Egyptian and Syrian participation in the American and British destruction of Iraq and the calvary of its people.

## Notes

1. Middle East Watch, 7 March 1991. Articles 16 and 17 of the First Geneva Convention list the types of information required to be forwarded to families after identification of dead.

2. Knut Royce's report in *Newsday*, 31 March 1991.

3. Samir al-Khalil, *Republic of Fear: The Politics of Modern Iraq*, University of California Press/Hutchinson Radius, 1989.

4. Michael Klare, 'Proche-Orient, une guerre de cent ans', *Le Monde Diplomatique*, March 1990.

5. *Washington Post*, 3 April 1991.

# ALEXANDER COCKBURN
## *and* ANDREW COHEN

## *The Unnecessary War*

The war is 'just', President George Bush declared to Congress, and he had been preceded to this moral eminence by the doyen of American liberal commentators, Anthony Lewis, who, after nine days of bombing, reassured his readers, 'It is a just war.' Set in the depthless present, amid fake-perspective murals of a bogus past, journalism in times of war is mostly moral persuasion of the citizenry that the war is fought by decent people for honourable objectives. The claim that war against Iraq was just followed from the premise that it was 'unavoidable', which in turn followed from the claim that neither had Saddam Hussein shown the slightest flexibility in heeding the calls of the United Nations, nor were economic sanctions showing signs of being successful in forcing him to do so. Just as carpet bombing is one means of waging war, so too, in the form of censorship, is denial. During the war in the Persian Gulf, it was denial that became the determining condition of all television and press coverage. The extent of Iraq's devastation – 'near apocalyptic' according to the United Nations Undersecretary-General's March 1991 report – was as absent from the American media as Saddam Hussein and the West's deals with him were before the war.

US policy first 'tilted' towards Iraq at the start of the 1980s and the new Republican administration of Ronald Reagan. To help Saddam Hussein win his eight-year war against Iran, the United States gave him satellite intelligence, helicopters, agricultural credits and naval protection in the Gulf. A US Navy vessel, the *Vincennes*, was able to shoot down an Iranian civilian airbus filled with innocent people because Americans were in the Gulf aiding Iraq.

The USA supported Iraq in this fashion, though it was perfectly aware of Saddam Hussein's abominations, as were the French, who lent him fighter-bombers, the Germans, who made him mustard gas, and the British, with whom he was a major trading partner. On March 7 1990 the UN Commission on Human Rights, in which the USA is very influential, decided not to take action on a proposal for an inquiry into human rights violations in Iraq.

In 1983, the Reagan Administration extended US agricultural credits to Iraq, removed it from a list of 'terrorist nations' which could not purchase civilian aircraft and other US goods and, in defiance of a Congressional arms embargo, began secretly shipping it weapons through third-party intermediaries. Such arms transfers were explicitly ruled out by the Arms Export Control Act. Nevertheless, in October that year, William Eagleton, then the senior US diplomat in Iraq, recommended that the US 'selectively lift restrictions on third-party transfers of US licensed military equipment to Iraq.' Such shipments were made through Egypt, Kuwait and Jordan, and provided Iraq with state-of-the-art Hawk anti-aircraft missiles, among other things.

There were further dealings as reported by such journalists as Murray Waas of the *Village Voice* and Knut Royce of *Newsday*. On three occasions, beginning in 1982, the Pentagon invited Iraq to swap American arms for Soviet technology. US defence planners were eager to procure Soviet T-72 tanks and Hind helicopters, in order to devise counter-weapons. With Defense Secretary Caspar Weinberger's approval, Iraq was first offered four American-made 155 mm howitzers in exchange for one new Soviet tank. Adnan

Khayrallah, the late Iraqi Minister of Defence, negotiated the deal but backed out at the last minute, fearing that the Soviets would discover the swap. A year later, in 1983, the Iraqi army was given the chance to purchase thirty American 175 mm guns, once again in exchange for a tank. US army general Richard Stilwell jacked up the price of the guns to $54 million at the last minute, and the Iraqis demurred. In March 1983 the Pentagon tried again, acting on a lead from Carl Perry, a senior executive of Hughes Helicopter. This time, the Iraqis were interested in swapping a Hind helicopter for US arms. The deal collapsed because Perry was fired from Hughes and subsequently indicted for trying to smuggle 103 Hughes combat helicopters fitted with Tow missiles to Iraq.

Perry's partner in such manoeuvres was a Lebanese-born arms broker named Sarkis Soghanalian, who went on to provide the Iraqis with 500 Russian-made surface-to-surface missiles and $1.4 billion worth of French howitzers. He was also instrumental in recruiting US army Major Charles Michael Chinn to help the Iraqis learn to pilot an F-4 jet they had captured from Iran. US air force intelligence officers apparently had full knowledge of Chinn's trip.

Such brokered deals were a staple of the United States's arms policy. Typically, as with the French howitzer sale, US allies were given back-channel encouragement to sell to Iraq. Besides the high-tech guns, France supplied 113 Mirage jet fighters and 880 Exocet air-to-surface missiles. (The French air force remained grounded during the Gulf War, because the Mirages were indistinguishable from the Iraqis'; the howitzers were used against Allied positions; and it was an Exocet missile that killed the thirty-seven American sailors aboard the USS *Stark* in 1987.) Since the first-aid packages under Giscard and Chirac, France had supplied Iraq with twelve to twenty billion dollars' worth of state-subsidized military hardware. France built the Osirak nuclear reactor in 1979 and promised to build another one after the first was bombed in 1981 (it never followed through on the promise). On 2 August

1990, a fifth of Saddam Hussein's arsenal was French. But it was the Russians who best outfitted him, supplying perhaps four times as many missiles and planes as the French. At least twenty German companies helped to arm Saddam Hussein, supplying most of the materials for Iraq's nerve and mustard gas production as well as components for a high-speed centrifuge necessary to purity uranium. Over a hundred German companies are still being investigated; in at least one case, trade continued in violation of the Security Council embargo. In a turn of events which is less menacing but more bizarre, Romania had earlier supplied the Iraqi army with uniforms after Richard Nixon sent his San Clemente chief of staff, Jack Brennan, to deliver a personal request to Nicolae Ceausescu.

Between 1982 and 1985, a programme called 'Operation Staunch' successfully discouraged Spanish, Portuguese, Italian, Argentine and South Korean arms sales to Iran. Around the same time the United States began to supply Iraq with 'dual-use' technology, mostly aircraft and electronics equipment that could be converted to military applications. In 1982 Iraq purchased sixty Hughes helicopters; an eyewitness account subsequently charged that they were being used to train military pilots. In 1984, the same year that the Reagan Administration moved to resume diplomatic relations with Iraq after a seventeen-year lapse, the State Department approved the sale of forty-five Bell 214 helicopters to Iraq. Soghanalian brokered the $107 million deal; George Schultz defended it, claiming that it served 'the United States's interest by improving our balance of trade, lessening unemployment in the aircraft industry'. In October 1988 a *Washington Post* reporter saw military pilots using the Bells.

This did not deter Reagan from signing a National Security Decision Directive, in June 1988, calling for closer American–Iraqi commercial relations. He relaxed controls on the export of technology. Two months later, Iraqi planes and helicopters dropped chemical weapons on Kurdish villages. George Schultz called the gassing 'unjustifiable and abhorrent'. The next day he helped defeat a trade sanctions bill that the Senate had passed.

After George Bush took office in 1988, the tilt became more pronounced. The Commerce Department approved more than a dozen exports to Iraq – including chemicals necessary for the manufacture of nerve gas. Commerce seems to have been acting on orders from the National Security Council.

Bush's Iraq policy was set down cogently enough in National Security Directive 26, signed in October 1989. NSD-26 was to the point: 'the United States remains committed to defend its vital interests in the [Gulf] region, if necessary and appropriate through the use of US military force, against the Soviet Union or any other regional power with interests inimical to our own.' Not without some concern for Iraq's human-rights record, its interest in Lebanon, its chemical and biological weapons arsenal, and its nascent nuclear programme, Bush's directive recommended more of the same. It argued that normal diplomatic relations, credit guarantees, and the participation of the US private sector in Iraq's postwar reconstruction would encourage Iraqi 'moderation' and promote 'stability' in the Gulf.

Bush's new policy directive stood its first test on 6 October 1989, when Iraqi Foreign Minister Tariq Aziz came to Washington to see US Secretary of State James Baker. Apparently, in a series of briefings with friendly Arab states, Central Command had identified Iraq as a potential threat to the Gulf region. Aziz was furious about this 'campaign' of hostility, but Baker reassured him. The two went on to discuss the renewal of US government credit guarantees for Iraqi food imports.

Since 1983 the USA had extended Commodity Credit Corporation (CCC) guarantees to Iraq annually, enabling it to buy more American agricultural exports than it could have otherwise. Such financing made Iraq America's third largest trading partner in the Middle East – after Israel and Saudi Arabia – (buying \$4.4

billions worth of goods in the first quarter of 1990), the single largest overseas consumer of US rice (the USA has sold Iraq as much as 20 per cent of its annual crop) and one of the largest importers of US corn, wheat, and other grains. In a sense, the Iraqis were on the receiving end of what the columnist James Ridgeway called 'a market-driven quest to relieve the Republican heartland' – the Iraqi trade helped Midwestern farmers to weather a depression that pushed down the price of farm commodities throughout the 1980s. It was not surprising, then, that in November 1989, after Baker had spoken to Aziz, Bush authorized $500 million in CCC credit guarantees. Iraq received $1.1 billion in fiscal year 1988; between 1985 and 1990 it received over $4 billion in US-guaranteed agricultural exports.

ON 17 January 1990, over Congressional objections, Bush reauthorized Export-Import Bank financing for Iraq's commercial transactions; this involved a $200 million dollar line of short-term non-payment insurance. Without such guarantees – that is, before 1987, when they were renegotiated – Iraq was considered a major credit risk. American-owned banks have lent it only $100 million to date; for eighteen months it was in default on Export-Import Bank loans. The Reagan Administration allowed Iraq and the Eximbank to settle their differences, just in the nick of time. By the end of the war with Iran in 1988, Iraq owed $80 billion, 1.5 times its Gross National Product. Short-term loans from Europe, Japan and the United States accounted for $30 billion, payable only in hard currency. Iraq's cash reserves were low, its oil profits eaten up by falling world prices and interest payments on its debt. According to Henry Gonzalez, chairman of the House Banking Committee, the Commodity Credit Corporation and Eximbank credits saved Iraq from bankruptcy. Iraq was still a credit risk, but the US government, which chose to finance it, was not. American corporations were eager for a piece of the action; according to one Eximbank official, 'we cautiously opened in Iraq only for short-term insurance despite *tremendous* pressure from the American business community.' And as Gonzalez went on to say, Iraq

> often threatened to default on its official debts if a nation would not reschedule its loans ... Iraq refused to reschedule loans with nations in a multilateral forum, a process referred to as the Paris Club. While this was a violation of stated US policy, it was purportedly ignored because Iraq was for the most part current on its US debt.

The 'tremendous' pressures on the banking community to expand trade with Iraq, and on Congress to withhold sanctions, were due in good part to the efforts of the Washington-based US–Iraq Business Forum. In its prewar heyday, the Forum had over fifty corporate members, thanks in part to booming trade (from January to September 1989 exports to Iraq grew to over $900 million and US imports totalled $1.8 billion). The Iraqi ambassador also helped out, sending the Forum a note on embassy letterhead to distribute to American Chief Executive Officers (CEOs). It suggested, rather bluntly, that 'any United States company interested in doing business with Iraq ... would do well to join the Forum' – this before the said Forum even had an office. The Forum prospered. Officials of Amoco, Mobil, Westinghouse and the First City Bancorporation of Texas were given seats on its board of directors; its corporate affiliates expanded to include General Motors, AT&T, Bankers' Trust, Occidental Petroleum, and Pepsi-Cola International.

Forum president Marshall Wiley regularly opposed sanctions in letters to the *Washington Post* and in television appearances. In an October 1988 letter to President Reagan, Wiley urged: 'we fully understand and agree with your desire to limit the use of chemical weapons ... [but sanctions] would have the opposite effect.' In early 1989, Wiley organized a trip to Iraq for Chief Executive Officers of twenty-three of the largest firms in the USA. They were given a special two-hour audience with Saddam Hussein. Bell Helicopter, Amoco, General Motors, Caltex and Mobil executives were all on hand, along with Alan Stoga of Kissinger Associates. Much has been made of the Kissinger connection, but Bush adviser Richard Fairfield, who served as one of the five top officers of the Forum, illustrates the business/diplomacy overlap most clearly. Despite Iraq's dependence on the USA, its powerful (though unofficial) lobby, and his own directive, Bush was apparently reluctant to expand US credits to Iraq in 1990 for two reasons. One was that soon after his Export-Import Bank decision, in February 1990, the State Department would issue its Human Rights Report. The report called Iraq's record 'abysmal' and documented the attacks on Kurdish villages which left thousands dead and 65,000 refugees. The second reason was that some troubling 'irregularities' in Iraq's use of CCC funds had come to light.

On 4 August 1989, Federal Reserve investigators, the FBI and the US Attorney raided the Atlanta agency of Banca Nazionale del Lavoro (BNL). They discovered that over $3 billion of unauthorized loans to Iraq had been kept off the books. They also found apparent irregularities in the legitimate CCC-insured dealings BNL had handled for Iraq. After the raid, the Department of Agriculture was alerted to the problems: the 'unusually high prices obtained by exporters' doing business with Iraq, Iraq's 'utilization of after-sales services', and its requirement that exporters pay a stamp tax. As one commentator put it in lay terms:

> Iraqi purchasing agents in Baghdad would badger American companies selling agricultural commodities to pay bribes ... In some instances companies would be asked to pay bills from suppliers of other types of goods. When Comet Rice, a big supplier, balked at paying $32,000 to a European parts company, thinking it might be paying for military parts, the Iraqis took

great affront, righteously pointing out that other grain companies had been asked for special payments and, by implication, made them.

The implication is that the difference between the real cost of commodities and 'the high prices paid by exporters' became a slush fund for Iraqi arms purchases.

Gonzalez has alleged that the Iraqis maintained a network of American front corporations in order to procure the latest Western military technology. His most specific example was the Cleveland-based machine tool company Matrix-Churchill, which supplied computer-controlled lathes and other machinery for Iraq's Taji Complex. Besides its role in the Taji Complex, Matrix-Churchill sought out US contractors to handle other Iraqi business. The US government happily granted export licences to a fibreglass manufacturer and a cutting-tool company they recruited. A team of German investigators subsequently discovered that the Taji Complex was in fact the Taji Cannon Complex, and was intended to manufacture gun barrels. In their turn, the Cleveland authorities discovered that Matrix-Churchill was Iraqi-owned; that its new procurement division operated in Arabic; and that its subcontractors were to manufacture fibreglass missile casings and tools with nuclear applications. Gonzalez claims: 'the US Customs service confiscated Matrix-Churchill in September 1990, calling it an "Iraqi front company".'

On a more mundane level, BNL loans helped Iraq to build a Pepsi-Cola bottling plant, import 10,000 Oldsmobiles, finance petrochemical plants and build the Badush dam. Whether US intelligence officials, corporate CEOs and bank regulators knew the funds were also being used to build guns and fund missile programmes remains unclear. Could the US intelligence community claim complete ignorance when over 3,000 telexes were sent between BNL and Iraqi government agencies?

By mid-January 1990, some people in the State Department began to argue that the United States's policy towards Iraq was flawed. On 11 February, one year after he was made Assistant Secretary of State for Near East and South Asian affairs, John Kelly was sent to Baghdad for the first time, for a cordial meeting with Saddam Hussein. Saddam Hussein mused on the end of the Cold War; Kelly broke the news that the State Department's Human Rights Report wasn't good press. That is where things stood until a few days later, at the 24 February Arab Co-operation Council summit in Jordan, where Saddam Hussein voiced his worry that with the decline of the USSR, the United States would behave in an 'undisciplined and irresponsible' manner and encourage Israel to embark on 'new stupidities'. He was particularly concerned with the influx of Soviet Jews to the occupied territories, and with the strength of the US fleet in the Gulf, augmented during the Iran–Iraq War. Saddam Hussein recommended that 'just as Israel controls interests to put pressure on the Administration, hundreds of billions invested by the Arabs in the United States and the West may be similarly deployed ... some of these investments may be diverted to the USSR and East European countries.'

Saddam Hussein was also upset by a Voice of America editorial, broadcast in Arabic on 15 February. It denounced the secret police forces of Iraq and seven other countries, and argued: 'the rulers of these countries hold power by force and fear, not by the consent of the governed ... the tide of history is against such rulers. The 1990s should belong not to the dictators and secret police, but to the people.' April Glaspie, US ambassador to Baghdad, cabled Washington that the Iraqi leadership had taken the broadcast to be US government 'sanctioned mudslinging with the intent to incite revolution'. She sent Saddam Hussein her regrets, along with the message: 'it is absolutely not United States policy to question the legitimacy of the government of Iraq nor interfere in any way with the domestic concerns of the Iraqi people and government.' Voice of America officials were rebuked by Baker and Kelly, and new procedures were set up so that the State Department had to give advance clearance for all VOA editorials dealing with Iraq.

Former Assistant Secretary of State for the Near East Richard Murphy made a business trip to Baghdad in early March. He had been engaged as an adviser by a California bank, and what he found alarmed him: Iraq's debts were piling up, its million-man army was still mobilized, and the Iraqi public was in a panic that an Israeli attack might be imminent. In early March the CIA detected the construction of six fixed, long-range Scud missile launchers near Iraq's Jordanian border. On 9 March, Iraq brought London *Observer* journalist Farzad Bazoft to trial on charges of spying for Israel; within a week, he was executed. Later that month, the Mossad assassinated Gerald Bull, a naturalized American who designed Iraqi artillery; US and British investigators also completed a 'sting' operation by arresting Iraqi agents who were trying to smuggle electronics back to Baghdad. Saddam Hussein's response, on 1 April, was to announce that Iraq had successfully developed binary chemical weapons. He then warned Israel that it had better not attack any more Iraqi plants. If attacked, Iraq would 'make the fire eat up half of Israel'. Later in the month he called for a conference to ban 'all weapons of mass destruction' in the Gulf region.

Saddam Hussein summoned Saudi Prince Bandar to convey his assurances to George Bush and Margaret Thatcher that he had no plans to attack Israel. He sought guarantees that he would not be attacked. The response was cool. Bush was still upset about the 'burn Israel' speech. 'Why does he say these things?' he asked Bandar.

Soon after this, on 12 April, a delegation headed by Senator Robert Dole arrived in Mosul. Saddam Hussein complained once more of a campaign of US hostility, upset that the USA had sold Israel Patriot missiles. Senator Dole, concerned about the long term, not to mention the grain exports of his native state, Kansas, assured Saddam Hussein that the President would veto any sanctions Congress tried to impose on Iraq.

16 April marked the first formal meeting of the Deputies Committee, an inter-agency group one level below the National Security Council in the administration hierarchy. Although the NSC never had a meeting about Iraq, the Deputies Committee had two formal meetings and several informal ones, all chaired by departing National Security Adviser Robert Gates. At this first formal session, Undersecretary of State Robert Kimmitt argued that Iraq's CCC and Export-Import Bank aid should be cut off. He was opposed by others at the meeting who believed that such actions would only end up 'hurting US rice producers'. According to an internal Department of Commerce memo, Dennis Kloske, Undersecretary for the Bureau of Export Administration, was also present at both formal Deputies meetings, arguing for stricter control on exports with potential military applications. By the second formal meeting on 29 May it was clear that Iraq would receive no additional credit incentives. Saddam Hussein would claim, subsequently, that the USA wanted to starve the Iraqis; and in Geneva Tariq Aziz would bitterly remind James Baker that

> the United States actually implemented an embargo on Iraq before August 2, 1990. We had dealings with the US in the field of foodstuffs; we used to buy more than a billion dollars of American products. Early in 1990, the American Administration suspended that deal, which was profitable for both sides. Then the US government decided to deny Iraq the purchase of a very large list of items.

John Kelly acknowledged the 'deterioration' in US–Iraqi relations in his testimony before Congress on 26 April. Tom Lantos, a California Democrat, said it 'boggled' his mind that Kelly could persist in the hope that Iraq could become a 'peace-loving and constructive member of the international community'. 'At what point will the Administration recognize that this [Saddam Hussein] is not a nice guy?' he asked. Kelly had praised Saddam Hussein for 'talking about a new constitution and an expansion of participatory democracy'.

At the Arab League summit on 30 May, Saddam Hussein reportedly told the Kuwaiti emir, 'You are wrecking our means of sustenance, and if you cut people's means of sustenance, it is equivalent to cutting their neck.' He demanded reparations for Kuwaiti drilling in the Rumailah oilfield; Sheik Jamir Ahmed Sabah wouldn't budge.

On 16 July Tariq Aziz sent a letter to the Arab League, accusing Kuwait of stealing $2.4 billion worth of Iraqi oil and of exceeding OPEC production quotas. On 17 July Saddam Hussein accused Kuwait of stabbing Iraq with a 'poison dagger', and warned that 'something must be done'. The US Embassy in Baghdad and the State Department formally requested clarification every day for the next week. On 20 July a foreign attaché in Iraq reported considerable southward troop movements. No attempt was made to conceal them from passing foreign diplomats or anybody else.

That same day, Kuwait went on alert. The following day, the United Arab Emirates requested a show of US military support. The Pentagon dispatched six warships and arranged for a joint jet-refuelling exercise with the UAE on 23 July. The Saudis were invited to participate, but demurred. Robert Kimmitt suggested a more substantial show of force, but the Pentagon decided against it. When State Department spokesperson Margaret Tutwiler announced the exercise, she called for a peaceful settlement of the Iraq–Kuwaiti dispute. But in response to a question, she said, 'there are no special defence or security commitments to Kuwait.'

On 24 July, after meeting Saddam Hussein, Egyptian President Hosni Mubarak said that the Iraqis had 'no intention' of invading Kuwait and were only trying to frighten it into decreasing its oil production at the forthcoming OPEC meeting in Geneva. According to King Husain of Jordan, he was furious that Mubarak had leaked what was told to him in confidence. An Arab mini-summit was scheduled in Saudi Arabia for 31 July; Saddam Hussein, King Fahd and the emir of Kuwait would meet in Jeddah to discuss the border conflict, levels of oil production and the reduction of Iraq's war debt. The Kuwaitis and the Saudis had subsequently claimed to have pledged in principle to pledge billions of dollars to rebuild Iraq. There was some indication, before this, that Kuwait had been overproducing oil to put economic pressure on Iraq and gain leverage on the border issue; but after Mubarak's leak the Kuwaitis decided to call Saddam Hussein's bluff at Jeddah. They offered him only $500,000.

On 25 July April Glaspie delivered Tutwiler's statement to Deputy Foreign Minister Nizar Hamdoon in Baghdad. Shortly afterwards, Saddam Hussein summoned her. It was their first private meeting in Glaspie's two years as ambassador.

In early September the Iraqis released their English translation – seventeen foolscap pages – of the session between Saddam Hussein and April Glaspie. It was not so much a conversation as a robust monologue by Saddam Hussein, mustering coherent arguments against Kuwait and stating his intention to do something to alter the distressing situation.

Saddam Hussein: 'But when planned and deliberate policy forces the price of oil down without good commercial reasons, then that means another war against Iraq. Because military war kills people by bleeding them. And economic war kills their humanity by depriving them of their chance to have a good standard of living. As you know, we gave rivers of blood in a war that lasted eight years, but we did not lose our humanity. Iraqis have a right to live proudly; we do not accept that anyone could injure Iraqi pride or the Iraqi right to have high standards of living.' (This description of economic warfare closely echoes the bellicose prose of US campus strategists like Robert Tucker in the early 1970s, who urged military strikes against the oil sheiks.)

Saddam Hussein returned again and again to the price of oil, at one point saying that $25 a barrel is 'not a high price', to which

Glaspie remarked, 'We have many Americans who would like to see the price go above $25 because they come from oil-producing states.' Then she averred that the United States had 'no opinion on the Arab–Arab conflicts, like your border disagreement with Kuwait' and that 'James Baker has directed our official spokesman to emphasize this.'

As the session drew to a close, Glaspie put the question plainly: 'I received an instruction to ask you, in the spirit of friendship – not in the spirit of confrontation – regarding your intentions.' Saddam Hussein responded by saying that Iraq wanted a just solution but that its patience was running out. By the weekend (July 28–29) he would meet the Kuwaitis again: 'When we meet and when we see that there is hope, then nothing will happen. But if we are unable to find a solution, then it will be natural that Iraq will not accept death, even though wisdom is above everything else. There you have good news.' In other words, he hinted strongly at war and Glaspie was noncommittal, though friendly.

The following day *The Washington Post* carried a report on the Gulf crisis by Patrick Tyler in which he reported that 'some [White House, State *and* Department of Defense] officials asserted yesterday that an Iraqi attack on Kuwait would not draw a US military response, but the United States would join in condemning such a move and would work diplomatically to force Iraq's withdrawal.'

When the Iraqis released the transcript, it was not formally disputed by the State Department. By this time Glaspie was back in Washington, and declined all requests for interviews. In late March 1991 she finally testified before a Senate Committee and asserted that the Iraqi transcript had omitted her strong warnings that the United States would act to protect its vital interests. The Senators did not press her, nor subpoena her cable to Washington following her meeting with Saddam Hussein, even though senior State Department officials suggested that the Iraqi transcript was essentially correct.

Certainly, Glaspie's line with Saddam Hussein was echoed by

her superior, in a venue where there could be no dispute about the accuracy of the record.

On 31 July 1990 John Kelly walked into the Rayburn building to testify before the Middle East subcommittee of the House Foreign Affairs Committee.

After Kelly's formal statement, Chairman Lee Hamiilton began to press him. Hamilton had read 'an indirect quotation in the press that Secretary of Defense Richard Cheney said that the United States's commitment was to come to Kuwait – to Kuwait's defence if it is attacked.' Was that statement accurate? Hamilton wondered. Could Kelly please clarify?

The following exchange may have launched a war and changed the face of the Middle East:

Kelly: I'm happy to, Mr Chairman. I'm not familiar with the quotation that you just referred to, but I am confident in the Administration's position on the issue. We have no defence treaty relationship with any Gulf country. That is clear. We support the security and independence of friendly states in the region. Ever since the Truman Administration we've maintained naval forces in the Gulf because of our interest in stability in that region. We are calling for a peaceful resolution of any differences in that area and we hope, and trust, and believe that the sovereignty of every state in the Gulf ought to be respected.

Hamilton: Now, do we have a commitment to our friends in the Gulf, in the event that they are engaged in oil or territorial disputes with their neighbours?

Kelly: As I said, Mr Chairman, we have no defence treaty relationships with any of the countries. We have historically avoided taking a position on border disputes or on internal OPEC deliberations, but we have certainly, as have all administrations, resoundingly called for the peaceful settlement of disputes and differences in the area.

Hamilton: If there – if Iraq, for example, charged across the border into Kuwait and – for whatever reason – what would be our position with regard to the use of US forces?

Kelly: That, Mr Chairman, is a hypothetical or a contingency question, the kind of which I can't get into. Suffice it to say we would be extremely concerned, but I cannot get into the realm of 'what if' answers.

Hamilton: In that circumstance, it is correct to say, however, that we do not have a treaty commitment which would obligate us to engage US forces there?

Kelly: That is correct.

This exchange did not go unnoticed. The next day, the *Financial Times*'s Washington correspondent was reporting to his London office apropos the Gulf crisis 'the one striking public statement, that the US has no defensive treaties with Kuwait or any of its neighbours'.

A report of this exchange went out on the BBC World Service and was no doubt reviewed with interest by Saddam Hussein, who was about thirty hours away from invading.

Unless one espouses the conspiracy theory that the United States wanted Iraq to invade Kuwait as an excuse to crush Saddam Hussein, then surely the simplest explanation is that the Bush Administration was trying to shove Kuwait into a more tractable posture with regard to the price of oil and possibly to the leasing of the two islands so desired by Iraq for the construction of a deep harbour in the Gulf. Iraq, after all, was a US ally and already a serious trading partner. Nor would the Administration, strongly orientated to the oil lobby, have been at all averse to seeing a hike in prices, which had drifted in real terms below their 1973 level. By seizing the whole of Kuwait, Saddam Hussein overplayed the hand allowed by the United States.

In fact by 25 July the CIA had decided that Saddam Hussein wasn't bluffing, predicting that he would confine himself to seizing disputed territory on the Kuwaiti border. Mubarak, Fahd and

Jordan's King Husain, meanwhile, did their best to discourage American intervention in the dispute. And in Baghdad Saddam Hussein's son-in-law, Hassan Kamal, asked April Glaspie's help in getting some export licences that the US Department of Commerce had blocked. She asked him about the troop build-up and he claimed that the troops would not be used. Two days later, and six days before the invasion, Republican Senators Robert Dole and Philip Gramm led an unsuccessful charge to expand Iraq's insurance and agricultural credits.

John Kelly called in Iraqi ambassador Mashat on 1 August to confront him with the CIA's estimate that an Iraqi offensive was imminent. Kimmitt chaired a final, informal session of the Deputies Committee because Gates was out of town.

For those who claim that there was no alternative to going to war, it is worth outlining the negotiating record before the commencement of hostilities. For obvious reasons, this record has been almost entirely suppressed on both sides of the Atlantic.

Even before Iraq made a first formal announcement of its broad negotiating posture on 12 August Deputy Foreign Minister Nizar Hamdoon communicated a proposal at the end of the first week in August for an Iraqi withdrawal in exchange for access to the Gulf via the islands of Bubaiyan and Warbah, plus negotiations on the price of oil. This was presented to Brent Scowcroft and National Security Council officials by 11 August. In the words of one of the intermediaries, former CIA chief Richard Helms, 'the US government didn't want to make a deal'. The peace feeler, as another participant in the talks with the NSC put it, 'was already moving against policy'. The following week, Iraq publicly proposed a Middle East Peace Conference to settle all regional conflicts – Kuwait, Palestine, the Lebanon. Of course, Saddam Hussein's motives for this, after his grab for Kuwait, were bad – but so what? Were US or Israeli motives, with decades of aggression and manipulation in the Middle East behind them, good? Such a conference would have been a perfectly acceptable way out of the crisis for anyone without double standards.

Saddam Hussein made his first 'linkage' proposal on 12 August in the course of a radio address:

> I propose that all cases of occupation, and those cases that have been portrayed as occupation, in the region, be resolved simultaneously and on the same principles and basis that should be laid down by the Security Council, as follows:
>
> Preparation for an immediate and unconditional Israeli withdrawal from occupied Arab lands in Palestine, Syria and Lebanon; a Syrian withdrawal from Lebanon; mutual withdrawals by Iraq and Iran and arrangement for the situation in Kuwait.
>
> All military withdrawals should take into consideration Iraq's historical territorial rights and guarantee the Kuwaiti people's right to decide on their future.

This was somewhat different from what was being said in the back-channel proposal. Again, according to Bob Parry,

> Hamdoon updated the plan on 23 August to include the release of all Western hostages and the lifting of United Nations sanctions against Iraq as well as requests for joint US–Iraqi efforts to improve stability in the Gulf and ease Iraq's economic problems.

The proposal failed to mention Palestinians or US troop withdrawals. Instead it offered to negotiate an oil agreement 'satisfactory to both nations' national security interests' and to 'jointly work on the stability in the Gulf'. The basic substance of the proposal was withdrawal in exchange for the long-term lease of uninhabited mudbanks at the mouth of the Shatt-al-Arab waterway and sole rights to the disputed oilfield which edged over the Kuwaiti border.

Knut Royce broke the story on 29 August in *Newsday*. On 30 August *The New York Times* quoted a Washington official who called reports of the proposal 'baloney'. It then admitted that the proposal did exist, that it 'had not been taken seriously because Mr. Bush demands the unconditional withdrawal of Iraq from Kuwait', and that a 'well-connected Middle Eastern diplomat told the *New York Times* a week ago [23 August] of a similar offer', but the *Times* suppressed the story.

The Bush administration seemingly had a timetable by 30 October that called for an air war in mid-January and a ground assault in February. On 21 October General Norman Schwarzkopf was sent to Saudi Arabia to sound out the offensive option; the decision was made to increase the US forces in the Gulf, but kept secret until two days after the election.

In late November, Bush went through the motions of going 'the extra mile for peace,' offering to send Baker to Baghdad to meet with Saddam at a 'convenient time between 15th December and 15th January'. Iraq accepted the invitation 'with surprise and enthusiasm', according to the *Times*. Within a week, citing 'good, positive changes', Saddam Hussein released all the hostages and invited Baker to Baghdad on 12th January. The Bush administration then rejected this date because it was too close to the UN deadline, a switch Iraqi officials considered humiliating. The war proceeded on schedule, the bombs hitting Baghdad only days after the time of the proposed meeting. As King Husain said, just before the ground offensive.

> It is fairly obvious the infrastructure of the whole country [Iraq] has been destroyed ... I've been convinced for a while that there was no effort to dialogue, there was no effort to reach for a diplomatic solution, and there was preparation from the word go for war.

Around the turn of the year Iraq offered to withdraw from Kuwait if the United States pledged not to attack as soldiers were pulled

out, if foreign troops left the region, and if the~~ ~~
the Palestinian problem and on the banning of al~~ ~~
destruction in the region. This proposal was relaye~~ ~~
House by Yugoslav emissaries in the Non-Aligned Mo~~ ~~
duly rejected.

Thus it may be technically true to say that, before 15 F~~ ~~y
1991, Iraq had never used the word 'withdraw' in a public state~~m~~ent
concerning its presence in Kuwait; but it is also plain from the
foregoing overtures – acknowledged as such by the White House –
that, almost from the start, it has clearly recognized withdrawal as
being central to any peaceful settlement. Indeed, if we are to believe
accounts offered by intimates of King Husain of Jordan and of
Yasser Arafat, Saddam Hussein had agreed immediately after the
invasion to withdraw from Kuwait as long as the Arab summit
scheduled for 3 or 4 August forebore from criticism of Iraq.
According to this version of accounts, Mubarak agreed to the deal,
but changed his mind and denounced Iraq when the USA offered
to write off billions of dollars of Egypt's debt.

Two other episodes are worth relating since they augment this
picture of a US government resolute on avoiding peaceful settlement and determined to seize the opportunities offered by Saddam
Hussein's precipitate and entirely reprehensible invasion.

On 5 August Saddam Hussein summoned Joe Wilson, the US
charge d'affaires in Baghdad, to tell him that Iraq planned no
invasion of Saudi Arabia. Wilson subsequently confided that his
credibility with Saddam Hussein was blown. He had relayed
Saddam Hussein's pledge on Saudi Arabia to the State Department, only to read in a 6 August story by Patrick Tyler in the
*Washington Post*, faxed to him the next day, that he had supposedly
cabled the State Department an account of a meeting with Saddam
Hussein in which the Iraqi leader had said he would invade Saudi
Arabia if the Iraqi pipeline was cut.

In other words, within moments of the invasion, a faction within
US policy-making circles, determined to press forward to war and
to the destruction of Iraq as a regional power, was already

...ng the record with diligence and success. There are also
...ounts that, in his first trip to persuade King Fahd to accept US
troops, US Defense Secretary Richard Cheney used satellite
photographs selected to demonstrate an Iraq poised for invasion,
whereas subsequent photographs refuted such claims.

US diplomacy thereafter was a matter of avoiding a peaceful
settlement at all costs, just as Nixon and Kissinger avoided one in
the Paris talks with the Vietnamese in 1972. Despite the fact that
terms had been agreed in Paris in October 1972, it became US
policy to punish North Vietnam with Christmas bombing raids, at
the end of which – and after high losses of B-52s – Kissinger
returned to the negotiating table in January to extort, as he claimed
it, terms that had already been agreed in October. The terms were
agreed once more, but the USA continued to claim Vietnamese
'intransigence' and went on 'punishing' Vietnam for another two
years.


What of sanctions? Bush and his British subordinate maintained
that sanctions, which were imposed without any attempt at negotiations, could never have worked. As almost everyone subsequently
conceded, they were given no chance to do so, since the American
desire was for a military showdown all along. Just as the sequence
of negotiating proposals was almost entirely suppressed in the
West, so too did Bush and his supporters assert after the bombing
began that sanctions were not effective, could never have been
effective. How could they know? Was it to be believed that leakage
of a few supplies over Iraq's land borders with its (highly hostile)
neighbours would have sustained Saddam Hussein over a period
of years? It can be argued, with better evidence, that sanctions
helped prompt him towards a negotiating table at which the
Americans were resolved not to sit.

Many liberal and even left intellectuals who should have known
better shared Bush's impatience with sanctions. The British academic Norman Geras, for example, in the war's aftermath made a

the October hearing transcripts and the February staff report of the House Committee on Banking, Finance and Urban Affairs, which Gonzalez chairs. See *Associated Press* reports by David Pace (14-2-91), Ruth Sinai (22-2-91) Marc Rice (26-2-91), James Rowley (28-2-91), David Page (6-3-91), and Dave Skidmore (9-10-90, 16-10-90, 11-3-91); also the *Financial Times* (Alan Friedman, (17-10-90, 30-1-91), *La Repubblica* (17 October 1990), the *New York Times* (Martin Tolchin, 10-10-90), the *Wall Street Journal* (Paul Duke, 10-10-90, 4-1-91), David Rubinger's recent series in the *Atlanta Business Chronicle*, the *Philadelphia Inquirer* (Barbara Demick and Matthew Purdy, 10-2-91), and the *Village Voice* (James Ridgeway, 12-3-91).

The *Voice* also had an excellent series of articles on the war. See Murray Waas (18-12-90, 22-1-91) and Michael Emery (5-3-91) for details of Saddam Hussein's stockpile and US–Arab relations before the conflict. For further details on the backchannel communications before the war, look for Knut Royce's pieces in *New York Newsday* (29-8-90, 3-1-91), Noam Chomsky in *Z* (12-10-90), and Bob Parry in *The Nation* (15-4-91). A broad overview of the events before 2 August is given in Don Oberdorfer's piece in the *Washington Post Magazine* (17-3-91).

Joe Conason described the Business Forum in the *New Republic* on 1 October 1990; he and Kissinger had an exchange in the letters column two weeks later. Jane Kramer wrote about the Amitiés Franco-Irakiennes, and the French dealings with Saddam Hussein in the 18 March *New Yorker*; *Der Spiegel*'s coverage of the German connection is by far the best (*Spiegel* 28/1990, 37/1990, 40/1990). Finally, Scott Henson, in the *Texas Observer* (25-1-91), provided a short history of the US military buildup in the Gulf and the Saudi quid pro quo.

# FALEH' ABD AL JABAR

## *Roots of an Adventure*
## *The Invasion of Kuwait:*
## *Iraqi Political Dynamics*

**1**5 January, 1991 will go down in history as the most outstanding and tragic event beginning the last decade of the twentieth century, at a moment when the old bipolar world system was disintegrating and supposedly being replaced by a more balanced multipolar system.

The factors behind the invasion and annexation of Kuwait are a mixture of domestic-Iraqi, regional and international phenomena, but the most important are the Iraqi internal dynamics. To simplify the presentation, I have divided this chapter into sections – first a general introduction covering 1968–80, then a section on the 1980–8 war against Iran, and finally the ramified consequences of these periods, which interacted during 1988–90 to produce the adventure of Kuwait.

## I

For the second time in the modern history of the country, the Iraqi Ba'ath Party seized power on 17 July 1968, relying on a group of officers from Takrit, Anna and other Sunni townships.[1]

Thirteen days later, two prominent non-Ba'athist officers, who had enabled the Ba'ath Party to assume power easily, were ousted: Ibrahim al Dawood, now in Saudia Arabia, and Abzul Razak al Naif, later assassinated by the Iraqi security service in London. At that time the Ba'ath Party had only 400–500 members, headed by the retired general Ahmad Hassan al Bakr and his assistant, a civilian deputy named Saddam Hussein, both from a small town north of Baghdad – Takrit.

Four political powers challenged the notorious and feeble Ba'ath Party. First, the rival left-wing pro-Syrian splinter group of the Ba'ath Party itself. Second, the Iraqi Communist Party central command, a splinter group which opted for guerrilla warfare on the Guevara model. Third, the Kurdistan Democratic Party (KDP) fighting for the national rights of the Kurds; and fourth, the 'official' Communist Party, still influential in urban centres and the countryside.

To keep a firm grip on power, the ruling Party had to start a new page – 'a white revolution'.[2] As the Communists were tamed and an alliance with the KDP was forged, a campaign was unleashed against the dissident Ba'ath and the CP central command.

Later, in 1975, it was the turn of the KDP to be smashed – but not before the ground had been prepared for such a precarious move.

First, an autonomy agreement for Kurdistan was concluded on 11 March 1970; next, in 1972, foreign oil companies were nation-alized; then, in 1973, an alliance with the Communist Party was signed, backed by an earlier treaty of friendship with the Soviet Union.

By these measures the Ba'ath Party gained considerable popular-ity and muscle, but not enough to secure an easy victory over the Kurds, who were backed by a regional power, the Shah of Iran. But that alliance was not to last. The 1975 Iraq-Iran agreement on the Shatt-al-Arab waterway dealt the final blow to Kurdish hopes.

From 1975 onwards, Iraqi political life hinged on two rival poles: the Communists and the ruling Ba'athists. The latter adopted much of its rival's programme and, embarking on land reform and enlarging the state-run economic sector, claimed these as 'socialist transformations'. Growing oil revenues, political demagogy, and above all brutal persecution and pressure enhanced the power of the Ba'ath Party, and by 1976 its membership had reached one million.

## II

Ba'athist ideology is a combination of mystical and nationalistic dogmas formulated by a group of Syrian middle-class intellectuals such as al Arsouzi, Akram Hourani and Michel Aflaq. The latter relied heavily on the ideas of the French thinker Renan. Sati'i al Hasri, another theoretician of Arab nationalism, based his ideas on the classic German philosophy of Fichte and Hegel, which saw the spirit of the nation as incarnated in the language.

The aims of the Ba'ath Party are: (1) Arab unity; (2) freedom; (3) socialism. None of these should be taken literally. If Arab unity means creating an Arab nation-state extending from the Atlantic Ocean to the Gulf, freedom, according to the writings of Aflaq, is not democratic institutions but some sort of *spiritual* emancipation. As for their so-called socialism, it is presented vaguely as some sort of human justice.

This ideology was formulated during the 1940s to face the challenges of Marxism and traditional Islamic thought. Different interpretations of its content led to fierce internecine struggle and fragmentation.

In Iraq, however, the Ba'ath party built a specific type of *capitalism* (usually termed 'modernization'), characteristic of almost all backward countries which so belatedly embarked on capitalist-style development: *state capitalism*.[3]

Here the state acts as *collective* capital – that is, as collective owner and producer. As some economists put it, the state was, and to a great extent still is, the greatest single employer in terms of the number of its employees and the size of the capital it commands, etc.[4]

If modern civil society created the modern state in Europe, in our region it is the state that is creating civil society. The inverted relations between the two created the very basis of the omnipotent hegemony of the one-party or one-family rule system, or a mixture of both. This was the case not only in Iraq but also in Syria, Egypt, Iran, Tunisia, Sudan and elsewhere.

The dictatorial system in Iraq was, ironically, modelled on both Nazi and Stalinist ideas.[5] One-party rule was gradually built and institutionalized. It is irrelevant to depict the tyranny of this regime; suffice it to say that it has been a 'wonderland of terror'.

In the Arab world, the Ba'ath encountered two challenges – the rival Syrian Ba'ath and Gamal Abdel Nasser of Egypt. The first split and weakened; the second set the scene for Anwar Sadat. When Sadat made his peace with the Israelis, Baghdad's ambitions to assume *leadership* of the Arab world grew stronger. Iraq's oil wealth, relative military might and large population, combined with its seemingly stable society and the leadership vacuum in the Arab world, all intensified its drive for supremacy. In 1978 the first Arab Summit in Baghdad was convened to oppose Sadat's plan for peace with the USA and Israel. Iraq had already given up its revolutionary jargon for a more moderate form of Arabism, to calm the fears of the Gulf Emirs and Sheiks.[6]

Two events changed the course of Iraq's destiny – one internal, the other regional.

The internal event took place in 1977, when the seemingly tranquil political landscape was troubled by massive demonstrations in Najaf and Karballa and other Shiite townships, long before the name of Khomeini was in circulation. When Khomeini came out victorious, the Da'wa Party, which had led the 1979 demonstrations, re-emerged to challenge Ba'ath hegemony. In both cases, the protesters were drowned in blood.

In 1979 – after a long and bloody mass struggle – the Shah of Iran's regime collapsed, and Ayatollah Khomeini, the religious leader who had spent the last sixteen years in exile in Iraq, assumed power. The emergence of a 'revolutionary' and Islamic republic fashioned on Ayatollah Khomeini's ideas of Shiite jurisprudence was a nightmare not only for the USA and the Gulf States, but also for Iraq.

This event taught a bitter but instructive lesson: how unnamed masses could topple a one-party, one-family tyranny. Iraq and Iran were both oil-producing countries – both had one-party rule:

Ba'ath and Rastakhiz ruled their country with an iron fist; both had a rebellious Kurdish population; and both faced fundamentalist Shiite organizations: the Da'wa Party in Iraq, presumably organized by Ayatollah Muhamed Bakr al Sadir, and in Iran the Khomeini movement, which eventually assumed power. Like the Iraqi Ba'ath in the early 1970s, the new Iranian leadership – acting as they thought, on behalf of the Deity – were bent on spreading the word of God – that is, exporting the Islamic revolution.[7]

1979, the year of the Iranian revolution, was a difficult period for the Shiite opposition. Saddam Hussein took power from the ageing Ahmad Hassan al Bakr, and Ayatollah Muhamed Bakr al Sadir was executed. War between Iran and Iraq was inevitable.[8] It was planned to take six days, but it lasted eight years; it was fought at the beginning under Arab slogans and ended with Iraq paying lip service to the cause of peace. The whole episode was a reminder of what Napoleon Bonaparte said after his ordeal in Spain: never invade a country in rebellion!

## III

On 20 August 1988, the most horrible war in the history of Iraq came to an end when Iran, in the words of Ayatollah Khomeini, drank the cup of poison and accepted UN Resolution 598. A new era had started.

The war had resulted in many contradictions. Iraq had emerged a mighty military power in terms of equipment and the number of men under arms, but it was economically bankrupt. Internally, the social fabric was overstretched. Externally, Arabs welcomed Iraq's might as a counterweight against Israel, while the USA and Israel were alarmed by it. Gulf rulers who were protected against Iranian expansionism became uneasily aware that their patron might well turn into their persecutor.

But internal problems were the main concern of Saddam Hussein's regime. Iraq had lost 300,000 lives in the war with Iran, with a million injured and maimed. It spent more than $130 billion and had to pay around $63 billion for reconstruction projects.[9] This not only consumed around $40 billion of Iraq's revenues but forced it to ask for credits of $85 billion, half of it from the Gulf States, notably Kuwait and Saudi Arabia.

During the war, more than three-quarters of a million Iraqis, mostly Shiites, were forcibly deported and their property was confiscated. A similar number fled into exile to evade persecution. Millions of Kurds suffered under constant security service terror campaigns. Their villages were razed and attacked with chemical and conventional weapons, thousands were evacuated from their areas and thousands were executed. Political tyranny, ethnic oppression, religious and sectarian persecution and an acute economic crisis fuelled by the deterioration of agricultural and industrial production overshadowed the country.

Living standards also were rapidly deteriorating: for the workers whose trade unions had been abolished, for the peasants whose land was being confiscated, and for the vast majority of the lower-middle classes who were abruptly marginalized.

Meanwhile, a precarious cease-fire with Iran reigned within the context of a no-war-no-peace situation. The war itself, though victory was claimed, ended where it had begun – with negotiation over the Shatt-al-Arab waterway, a problem that could have been negotiable eight years earlier by peaceful means. But if war had ignited a host of contradictions, it had also brought about other counterfactors.

First, it had furnished the regime with a powerful political weapon, *Iraqi patriotism*, which served not only to mask the internal wounds or make them endurable, but also to cover the mass terror campaign to annihilate hundreds of opposition activists, who were executed without much reaction from the international community.[10] This led to a paradox: inasmuch as the *discontent* was *growing*, the organized *structures* capable of mobilizing that discontent into *political action* were *diminishing*. In fact, all political parties were based abroad, in Damascus or elsewhere, or moved their headquarters and forces to the Kurdish mountains, as did the

Communists and the Kurdish parties. Islamic groups took shelter in Iran.

Nevertheless, Iraqi society was on the verge of exploding. But who would be the political 'agent' or 'historical subject' that would carry out the detonation?

The biggest problem for Saddam Hussein was not the opposition parties as such, but his own guardian, the army of one million men: How to keep it busy? How to feed it? After the cease-fire in 1988, he waged minor wars; the first was the chemical war against the Kurds; the second his roundabout war against Hafiz Assad of Syria at the hand of General Aoun in Lebanon; the third, perpetuated with knives and pistols, was the war against the Egyptian workers in Iraq. If revenge was sought in the first and second, the third revealed a tendency to throw economic problems on to the shoulders of outsiders.

In 1988–9, Saddam Hussein promised the angry soldiers that he would win the economic battle just as they had won military victory.

It was necessary to contain the growing social discontent, or at least channel it, so that the Iraqis could aim their angry fire at ghostly enemies. The economic problem, however, was too deep to solve with fervent words.

To keep his promise, Saddam Hussein started to sell state enterprises cheaply and *en masse* (his next-of-kin could buy the most profitable or have shares in them). Market powers were set free, though almost all Arab countries interfere, to various extents, in the operation of market mechanisms to reduce their negative effects, whether on the production level (providing facilities for private capital, for instance) or on the consumption level (subsidizing basic consumer goods). This phenomenon, seen in all Arab countries from the Atlantic Ocean to the Gulf, is considered economically imperative dictating state interference because of the low level of development.

The free-market economy proved disastrous. Prices soared, triggering fierce reactions, and price controls were re-introduced. New regulations to attract foreign and Arab investment were enacted, but did little to remedy the ailing Iraqi economy. The bloody crisis of street uprisings in neighbouring Jordan and in Algeria at the end of 1989 gave the Iraqi ruler yet another early-warning signal.

Unlike the economies of Jordan and Algeria, the Iraqi economy was suffering not only from a mixture of dwindling production and growing indebtedness, but also from huge military expenditure. In addition to feeding one million soldiers stationed on some 1,200 miles of the Iraq-Iran border, Iraq had allocated $22 billion to boosting the military industry. At a time of diminishing oil revenues, these investments were economic and social suicide.

In addition, the mass transformations in Eastern Europe from the one-party system to pluralism, coupled with a drive from centralized economy to market economy, dealt a severe blow to the very pillars of the Ba'athist ideology, partially based as it was on these dogmas, notably the legitimacy of the 'leading' role of the 'Party'.

The Iraqi and Syrian Ba'ath issued internal papers to their Party insiders, saying that Mikhail Gorbachev had betrayed revolutionary principles when he gave up the leading role of the Party, and that the revolutionary exception was Romania. The Romanian model was used as a showcase for years by the Ba'athists in Iraq, to emphasise the priority of nationalism over internationalism. When the Romanian dictator was captured and driven, like a wet mouse, into an armoured vehicle, to face the firing squad, his Iraqi counterpart distributed Ceausescu's photographs to remind his entourage of the consequences if and when they should desert their leader and dogmas. The wind of pluralism was too strong to resist, as it was drawing nearer, this time in the small emirate: Kuwait. Again, it was not the Kurds, the Communists or the Islamic Shi'ite parties that caused Saddam Hussein restless sleep during 1988–90 which, Iraqi opposition circles believe, were the two most difficult years of his entire period in power before the war.

The sociopolitical time bomb was the army. At least three, perhaps four generations had been recruited, driven to the battlefields, and kept there for almost a decade. They had suffered the horrors and agonies of a long and draining war, were deprived of the best years of youthful, active life, and became hungry for literally everything. In wartime, a sense of national obligation elevated their spirits; in a peacetime, longing for a lasting peace gathered momentum.

The army was the melting pot where all contradictions interacted. The Iraqi regime had two alternatives, the sweeter of which was bitter. To demobilize half the army would have been tantamount to setting that dangerous time bomb to work, but to keep them under arms would only delay rather than prevent the imminent explosion that even the Takriti hegemony in the army could do little to stop. If the 2,000 or so Takriti officers form a shield to protect the sensitive upper posts, they also constitute a barrier alienating the Takriti clan – the real backbone of the regime – from most junior officers and ordinary soldiers. This was Saddam Hussein's main problem after the cease-fire. To feed one million men under arms he needed cash, and to demobilize them he had to provide them with a decent living. Some 150,000 conscripts did return to civilian life but found little opportunity there, despite having been told that they were saviours of the Motherland, winners of a glorious victory, and Saddam Hussein's heroes. They proved to be a wild and uncontrollable political force between 1988 and 1990.

In a bid to control the uncontrollable, the notorious Iraqi penal code was enriched with a new death penalty for any verbal assault against the President – and that in a country whose people call God and all the Saints and Imams bad names at any moment of irritation. A new attempt was made to find a way out of the dilemma, and this time it was an offer totally alien to Saddam Hussein's spirit. Realizing that Iraqi society was stretched to its limits, he offered a complete package of reforms: economic liberalization coupled with political pluralism, press freedom and a new constitution. This conciliatory move was complemented by a similar burst of goodwill and an offer of real peace to the Iranian president Ali Akbar Hashimi Rafsanjani.

Behind this doveish show from a notorious hawk was a secret deal with Japanese companies (according to an opposition source) to sell out the oil reserves in the Majnoon Islands (in Ammara province, near the border with Iran), estimated to be around 33 billion barrels, for $180 billion, approximately 6 dollars per barrel. The grand contract needed two crucial preconditions: peace with Iran to render it operational, and internal political stability to ensure safety for such a long-term and costly enterprise.

Even without such a bargain, which would have had a far-reaching negative impact on the oil market, Iraq could have survived the economic hardships had a rational policy been pursued. The sane Dr Jekyll, however, invented the insane Mr Hyde. At the end of 1989 Iraq was at a crossroads: either to embark on peace and democracy, or to opt for continued expansion and terror – a mad alternative.

Four issues revealed the choice. First, the promised new constitution did not appear. When, secondly, Saddam Hussein was elected President for life, many opposition leaders considered it the death knell for domestic peace. Thirdly, military investments were increased, intensifying the already overstretched stresses on the Iraqi economy, not to mention the irritation and even mistrust they caused to the Iranian leadership. Fourthly, Iraq's establishment of the Arab Co-operation Council (ACC) with Egypt, Jordan and Yemen was meant not as an economic gathering, as was claimed,[11] but as a military pact that would trade its human and military weight for money. And of course the weak party that would pay for this was the Gulf Co-operation Council, a wealthy but thinly populated part of the Arab world, and hence the most vulnerable area in the region.

Baghdad's dreams of assuming the *leadership* of the Arab world were revived again, this time to be implemented with more militarization and within the framework of the ACC.

The Iraqi President learnt an important lesson from his Iranian adventure: that when war is launched it should be started *not* against charismatic leaders such as Khomeini, but against unpopular ones; and that it should be fast, decisive, apparently defensive and, lastly, undertaken for a noble and sublime cause.

The decision to invade Kuwait had been nourished since 1988, and the final plans, according to some Iraqi opposition leaders, were drawn up in March 1990 – long before the oil conspiracy (Iraq accused Kuwait of increasing production beyond the OPEC quota) was mentioned. In its annual meeting in March 1990, the central committee of the Iraqi Communist Party warned of Saddam Hussein's schemes in Kuwait. Kurdish leaders also warned world opinion. These warnings were based, according to a member of the central committee of the ICP, on a letter from an Iraqi insider confirming that plans to 'regain' Kuwait were in the making.

Saddam Hussein's regime was in desperate need of King Solomon's treasures in Kuwait – to boost its military projects on the one hand, and to relieve its economic woes on the other. No less important is the fact that war, especially a sweeping and victorious one, not only gives access to the wealth of the defeated but also triggers fanatical, *blind patriotism* that would presumably help to cement an almost worn-out social fabric. And of course, the road to Arab leadership would be clear.

The invasion and annexation of Kuwait was carefully preceded by a host of calculated measures: a non-aggression pact with Saudi Arabia; the launching of the first Iraqi missile into space, a symbol of the new Arab power; and finally the direct challenge to Israel that if it attacked Iraq, half of it would be burnt down.

For Saddam Hussein, the invasion took place at the right moment as far as the Arab world was concerned, because of the political weakness of all the Arab regimes which made it impossible for them to react; but at the worst moment as far as the international situation was concerned, because of the overwhelming US confidence in the post-Cold War era.

If he had planned to be the pre-eminent Arab leader, to hush up his opponents inside the country and to find a way out of economic hardship in order to continue his armaments projects, the whole episode ended in shambles on every front. There is a great conviction among Iraqi opposition leaders that the USA deliberately encouraged Saddam Hussein into Kuwait and hijacked the UN mandate for a multitude of reasons.[12] This will be a crucial matter in eventually determining the USA's real role in the conflict. Our main concern, however, is Saddam Hussein's policy, one based on domestic tyranny and expansionism abroad. The fact that the USA acted cynically does not in our view imply that Saddam Hussein was an innocent 'anti-imperialist' fighter.

The invasion of Kuwait was indeed carried out under popular slogans: Arab unity, a just distribution of wealth and the liberation of Palestine. In the first phase of the crisis, wide sections of the Arab people were actually attracted by these slogans. The questions they raised were true, but the answer was false, as Fred Halliday put it.[13] There was greater hatred for the Gulf sheiks and emirs, out of economic jealousy, than there was pure love for the Iraqi dictator. The frenzied US interference, compared with American indifference towards other regional problems, inflamed Arab enthusiasm for Iraq – not because of any merit Saddam Hussein might have, but because the image of the USA and the fear of Western hegemony are far more dangerous.

If the massive demonstrations in the Arab world and even beyond, in support of Iraq, revealed the deep-seated enmity towards the ex-colonial west, they also indicated to what extent wide sections of immature Arab masses, not to mention their leaders, longed for a great 'patriarch' – even if he is in his 'autumn', as the Colombian writer Gabriel García Márquez would have put it.

It would not be surprising if the defeat of Iraq revives rather than quells hopeful expectations of defeating the colonial West sometime and somehow in the future. This is a region whose poetic imagination is liable to turn the defeated into victors, which has the powers of fantasy that denied the death of the twelfth Shiite Imam, al'Mahdi. These might be dismissed as myths from antiquity, but the symbol they carry is a powerful political weapon created as a protective shield by hungry and illiterate masses whose intellectual irrationality is the creation of the rational West. It is a tragedy that the so-called modernizations carried out during the last twenty years have produced contradictory social and intellectual results, among which is the emergence of the fundamentalist movements, which flourished under the tyrannical one-party-rule system, and spread among illiterate and humiliated migrant masses who now live in shantytowns, bewildered, frustrated and ignorant. As the irrational product of rational modernization, these masses find their spiritual comfort in superstition and superstitious leaders. To avoid misuse of such sentiments by false saviours such as Saddam Hussein, democracy, economic development and national dignity for the region should be achieved – three vital aims for which the Iraqi people are still struggling.

## Notes

1. For more details, see Marion Farouk-Sluglett, *Iraq Since 1958*, London: I. B. Tauris, 1990, pp. 112, 116.

2. See *Saddam's Iraq, Revolution or Reaction, The Return of the Ba'ath July 1968*, London: Zed Books, 1989, p. 100.

3. See Tamas Szentes, *The Political Economy of Underdevelopment*, Budapest, 4th edn, 1989.

4. I. Khafaji, *State and Capitalist Development in Iraq* (Arabic edn), Cairo, 1983.

5. The 'leading role' of the Party in state and society is a Stalinist idea dearly loved by Saddam Hussein. The *unity* of the nation, the role of the *Führer*, the racial purity of the nation and the special message it carries, are part and parcel of Ba'ath thinking, derived from Nazi ideology. Germany was supported by some Arab nationalsim in the 1930s and 40s out of hatred for the British and French colonizers.

6. See Gerd Nonneman, *Iraq and the Arab States of the Gulf: Modified Continuity into the 1990s*, University of Exeter, 7 March 1989, pp. 1, 2.

7. A decade later, Saddam Hussein told Egyptian President Hosni Mubarak that Iran posed a more serious threat than Israel because Iran,

unlike Israel, had a powerful ideological weapon to 'penetrate Iraq' – namely, radicalized Shiism.

8. The Iraq-Iran political, ethnic and communal parallels and their impact on political life in Iraq in 1979–80 has been better illustrated in 'Baghdad Beats Drums of War, with an Eye on Counter-Revolution in Iran', in the monthly review *Al Thakafa Al Jadida*, Beirut, no. 116, 1979. This essay predicted that the war was looming.

9. All these and other figures are based on reports by the economic committee of the Iraqi Communist Party published in March 1989 in Damascus. They differ only slightly from other estimates put forward by some Iraqi and Arab economists.

10. To give one example: around 600 leftists were executed in 1987, among them many young women whom I knew. The details were cabled to humanitarian organizations, but the attention at that time was focused on the Battle of Foa, a small town south of Basra, which was occupied by the Iranians. The death toll on the Iraqi side was colossal: 15,000.

11. No concrete measures were taken to further trade between the member countries, let alone any serious step to lay down the pillars for a common Arab market, the absence of which is one of the main causes of economic backwardness in the region.

12. The meeting between Saddam Hussein and the US ambassador to Iraq, April Glaspie, days before the invasion, strengthened the impression that the Iraqi dictator was virtually encouraged into Kuwait. Glaspie kept silent during the critical times of the conflict. When it was over, she broke her long silence to tell Congress that she had warned Saddam Hussein but the warning paragraph was omitted from the text issued by the Iraqis, and insisted on the Iraqi President's *lack of credibility*. Of course Saddam Hussein is not credible, but why should that be a proof that *she* is credible? Both could be untruthful! She justified her silence by saying that had she talked, the coalition would have been disturbed.

Why should the Allies be disturbed if they came to know that Saddam Hussein was clearly warned? The French and other Europeans were for more political attempts; they were also suspicious of US intrigues. And if Ms Glaspie had confirmed the clear warning, that would have strengthened rather than weakened the US position in European eyes. During the negotiations between Iraq and Kuwait in late July the Kuwaitis were ready to pay $2.5 billion to Iraq for overproduction of oil, and to give territorial concessions on the Rumailah oilfields. Washington ordered them not to pay.

13.  In his essay 'The Crisis of the Arab World: The False Answers of Saddam Hussein', *Le Monde Diplomatique* (Arabic edn), November 1990, Fred Halliday rightly criticizes the Iraqi dictator, but there is not a single word about the USA's real intentions – namely, to control the oil-rich Gulf, and to impose a monopolar world system to replace the old bipolar one which had disintegrated rapidly by the end of 1989.

There was (and perhaps there still is) a great oversimplification of the conflict. Any criticism of Saddam Hussein was considered pro-USA, and any criticism of the USA was conceived as pro-Saddam Hussein.

No synthesis was attempted. This applies to both Arab and European left-wingers. As John Pilger pointed out (on 4 March 1990 – Media Workers' Meeting, London), the British MPs who had opposed Saddam Hussein's regime in previous years were the very ones who opposed the war in the Gulf, while all those who had been in favour of trade relations with Iraq were for the war. This is by no means a coincidence.

# Rear Admiral EUGENE J. CARROLL, Jr *and* Rear Admiral GENE R. LA ROCQUE

## *Victory in the Desert: Superior Technology or Brute Force?*
### Washington Center for Defense Information

### Background to War

The conduct of the Gulf War by a coalition of nations, dominated by the United States, will be analysed and debated for years to come. Although many facts remain unknown, it is vitally important to appraise what is currently known about the military conduct of the war. Accounts of war are often distorted by myths and emotion, by the winner as well as the loser. The sayings 'Truth is the first casualty in war' and 'Victors write the history books' may be clichés; none the less they are true.

From the US perspective, the war was particularly important in a number of respects. It was the first significant test of US military force in the post-Cold War world. Regardless of whether there truly is a new world order, the USA is likely to draw heavily on its experiences in this war as it reconfigures its armed forces for the future. In fact, Defense Secretary Richard Cheney has already instructed top Pentagon officials to conduct a review of 'lessons learned' during the Gulf War, including a technical assessment of how weapons performed in the conflict.

It was the first 'space war' in that it was heavily dependent on the wide array of orbiting satellites. It was the first significant test of new US military command and control arrangements brought about by the 1986 Goldwater–Nichols Defense Department Reorganization

Act which, among other things, gave more power to the leaders of unified commands, such as General Norman Schwarzkopf, and the Chairman of the Joint Chiefs of Staff, General Colin Powell. It was the first war in which many new, 'high-tech' weapons systems were used in combat. These included Patriot air defense missiles, Tomahawk cruise missiles, laser-guided 'smart' bombs, Apache attach helicopters, Bradley fighting vehicles and F-117A stealth fighters.

The initial Iraqi invasion in August 1990 was both swift and massive. Over 100,000 Iraqi troops, spearheaded by Republican Guard divisions, accompanied by 300 tanks, artillery, armoured personnel carriers and other supporting forces, crossed into Kuwaiti territory and within six hours occupied the country. Kuwait's military was no match for the superior Iraqi forces. The Kuwaiti army and air force put up only limited resistance before surrendering or escaping to Saudi Arabia.

On 5 August President Bush declared that Iraq's invasion of Kuwait 'will not stand'. Because of alleged concerns that Iraqi forces might invade Saudi Arabia to seize its oilfields, President Bush sent Defense Secretary Cheney to Saudi Arabia to persuade King Fahd to accept US forces.

The following day the USA began to expand its force of eight warships in the Middle East for a possible blockade to enforce trade sanctions. The Pentagon sent out rules of engagement for conducting naval intercepts of ships in violation a blockade, even though a blockade had not yet been approved by the UN. The aircraft carrier *Saratoga* and the battleship *Wisconsin* were sent to join the *Independence* carrier battle group which had arrived in the region. The *Eisenhower* aircraft carrier battle group was also ordered to the region, and by 8 August it had taken up a position in the Red Sea. Iraq began rounding up Westerners, including Americans, in Kuwait and taking them back to Iraq.

On 7 August President Bush announced that US armed forces were being sent to provide land, air and naval protection for Saudi Arabia. The deployment was named Operation Desert Shield to emphasize its 'wholly defensive' nature.

Since the end of the Vietnam War US military officials have examined and re-examined their military doctrines in the light of the failure to achieve a success in Vietnam. They have not only created and fielded new weapons but have devised new strategies and tactics. Professional military journals from all services have published explicit and candid articles about doctrines such as Air-Land Battle in which the goal would be the destruction of enemy combatants, not the seizure of territory. There would be no incremental tit-for-tat battles. War, if it came, would be swift, massive and incredibly violent. Emphasis would be placed on disrupting and destroying enemy forces through a combination of mobility, combined-arms operations, heavy use of information-processing technologies and advanced electronics, plus sophisticated munitions. In fighting Iraq the USA faced an opponent over which it had many advantages, including a sound doctrine and modern weapons.

Iraq's perceived main strength was sheer numbers. The published Pentagon estimate of Iraq's entire military force was one million, with an army of 955,000 men, which made it the world's fourth largest. It is now apparent that US intelligence grossly overestimated the actual size and combat readiness of the Iraqi forces. Originally US intelligence agencies estimated that Iraq had 545,000 troops in or near Kuwait at the start of the war. That number was based on the number of divisions sent. But since the war US military officials have said captured Iraqi soldiers claim that many divisions began the war badly undermanned and lost as many as half their troops to desertions at various points in the war. Reports from Iraqi prisoners of war suggest that approximately 350,000 Iraqi troops were in the Kuwaiti theatre at the beginning of the US air attack. More than 100,000 Iraqis may have deserted by the time the ground campaign began on 23 February, leaving fewer than 250,000 troops to face the massive attack by US and coalition forces.

The USA also had a vast superiority in communication and intelligence capabilities. The Gulf War was the first major US military action in which satellites played a significant role. Satellite communications systems were crucial for communication between the Pentagon and the Central Command in the Persian Gulf, and within the Central Command in Saudi Arabia. Information on enemy movements from military satellites provided early warning of enemy aircraft activity to assist the US commanders in directing the forces in the area. In some cases they were used to give Patriot missile batteries advance warning of incoming Scud attacks. Satellites also provided precise navigation data which proved critical in an often featureless desert environment. Weather forecasting vital for planning the thousands of air attacks was made easier by US satellite systems. Satellites also provided commanders with photographic and radar imagery and electronic intelligence. Terrain mapping by satellites also proved invaluable in programming the flight paths of Tomahawk cruise missiles launched from US warships and submarines.

A second major advantage the US commander had was the luxury of time. If Saddam Hussein's first mistake was in invading Kuwait, his second was in not promptly advancing into Saudi Arabia and seizing the modern ports and airfields which were essential to support the rapid deployment of US forces there. (Of course, Iraq's failure to take this action may be interpreted as indicating that its goals were more limited than President Bush and the Pentagon argued in August.) It is worth noting that the Saudis had spent tens of billions of dollars in recent years building up a modern infrastructure of military bases and transport networks. Almost all the new facilities were built by the US Army Corps of Engineers to American specifications; hence US forces felt completely at home when they arrived.

This brings us to America's third advantage: an enormous logistical capability. While the US military has often been criticized as being slow and cumbersome, its ability to provide the necessary weapons, ammunition, supplies and personnel, and move them across the world, is unequalled. When the histories of the war are written, much credit will be given to the logisticians who marshalled the ships and aircraft for transport, moved millions of tons of supplies and helped to integrate the forces of over thirty nations.

A fourth advantage from the very beginning of the deployment was the almost unlimited American airpower. Once the Americans had air superiority in the area they attacked at will, destroyed ammunition dumps, interdicted supply lines, eliminated command and control sites and killed Iraqi troops. Iraqi anti-aircraft artillery and surface-to-air missiles were only minor irritants. As General Powell said, 'First we will cut off the Iraqi army, then we will kill it.'

From the outset the Iraqis recognized that an air battle was futile. They kept most of their planes in hardened shelters and, somewhat unexpectedly and inexplicably, sent more than 100 of their best to Iran. They may have overestimated the extent to which their skill – acquired during their war with Iran – at building defensive fortifications would protect them from attack. And, although reliable information is not yet available, it is likely that they underestimated the effectiveness of some of the bombs that were used to destroy the shelters in which aeroplanes were parked.

Perhaps the biggest Iraqi weakness – which was not fully realized until the war was almost over – was the weariness of the armed forces. Many of Iraq's military personnel had been conscripted into service and had already served for several years. Iraq had just finished eight years of bitter war with Iran, and both soldiers and civilians demonstrated little enthusiasm for another war. One of Saddam Hussein's first actions after invading Kuwait was to give back Iranian territory Iraq had seized and held during the course of the previous war. This action could only have demoralized Iraqi troops who had won such territory at very high cost.

Another Iraqi failure was Saddam Hussein's attempt to weaken the coalition by inflaming anti-American sentiment in other Arab states. While there were significant demonstrations against Western military action, it is evident that many Arab states had no great affection for him and were happy to see his military power greatly reduced, if not utterly destroyed.

The USA steadily increased both the size and the capability of its forces after it first started Operation Desert Shield. It is now clear that the USA began preparing for offensive operations well before President Bush announced an increase in US forces on 8 November. In fact, even before that date the USA was deploying substantial air, land and naval forces far beyond that necessary to defend Saudi Arabia. US airpower in particular was clearly being readied for a massive assault against Iraq.

When President Bush made the 8 November announcement that he was deploying additional US forces in order to provide 'a credible offensive option', most of the media underestimated the extent of this deployment. Most news stories said it amounted to an effective doubling of US forces, raising the total to over 400,000 troops. On the first day of the war the US troop total was over 450,000. By 30 January 1991 there were over half a million US military persons in the area. By 20 February, shortly before the start of ground combat, more than 530,000 US forces were prepared for an attack against Iraq.

By the war's beginning on 16 January 1991 the composition of the US forces in the area were as follows:

Air force: Personnel 40,000; Fixed-wing aircraft 850 minimum. Total of fixed-wing aircraft from all services 1,680 minimum.

Navy: Personnel 70,000; ships 114; navy planes 530 (410 combat planes).

Army: Personnel 245,000 (approx. 70,000 of which came from Europe); main battle tanks 2,100.

Marine Corps: Personnel 100,000; Tanks 200.

Non-US coalition forces added about another 200,000 military personnel, primarily ground forces.

## Appraising the Air War

The Bush Administration moved quickly to create a powerful political, economic and military coalition opposed to Iraq. US leadership, with considerable pressure and persuasion, was largely exercised through the Security Council of the United Nations. US proposals were adopted in a series of resolutions which imposed various sanctions intended to punish Iraq for 'naked aggression'.

It was understood initially that sanctions would require patience to produce the withdrawal of Iraqi forces from Kuwait. As early as September 1990, however, the US government clearly set out to move beyond a wholly defensive military posture. On 8 November, two days after US national elections, President Bush revealed a plan to more than double US forces deployed against Iraq in order 'to create a credible offensive capability'.

The US build-up was paralleled by intense political pressure on UN Security Council members to approve the use of military force against Iraq and to set a deadline for the withdrawal of all Iraqi forces from Kuwait. US pressure ultimately produced a 12–2–1 vote for UN Resolution 678, authorizing 'all necessary means to uphold and implement Security Council Resolution 660 and all subsequent relevant Resolutions and to restore international peace and security in the area'. The deadline for Iraqi compliance was established as 15 January 1991. Just nineteen hours after expiration of that deadline, President Bush began the war against Iraq.

In the aftermath of hostilities, many legitimate questions have been raised concerning American actions in the war. Chief among these questions is whether the USA conducted attacks that went beyond the letter of Resolution 678, which authorized only appropriate measures to implement other relevant UN resolutions. These questions have been intensified since the war ended by reports of devastation in Iraq so extreme that UN Undersecretary General Martti Ahtisaari reported in March that bombing had pushed Iraq back to 'a pre-industrial age'. Reports from US military sources of more than 100,000 Iraqi military deaths have added to the controversy.

Nowhere in UN resolutions can any authority be found to attack the state of Iraq in order to weaken the economic or political fabric of the nation, nor to bring about the collapse of the Saddam Hussein government. Did, in fact, the US government conduct military operations in ways which extended, or exceeded, the formal authority granted in UN resolutions?

One way to address this question is to analyse the conduct of the five-week US air war against Iraq. Another event which was also revealing was the destruction of Iraqi forces withdrawing from Kuwait along the so-called 'Highway of Death' on 25 and 26 February.

A good case can be made that the air war against Iraq was brilliantly conceived and executed in support of UN resolutions. There can be no doubt that the first objective of the air war, defeat of the Iraqi air forces and destruction of their air defence system, was a valid military goal. To accomplish this task required repeated attacks against Iraqi air bases, command centres, radar and communication installations, anti-aircraft missile and artillery sites and aviation fuel supplies wherever located in Iraq. A sustained campaign against Scud launchers was also necessary.

The early establishment of coalition air supremacy then permitted a shift in priorities to targets more directly related to Iraqi forces in or near Kuwait. A sustained series of attacks on those forces was clearly justified in order to reduce the means by which Iraq could sustain its military position in Kuwait. Furthermore, as later events proved, the attacks clearly weakened the Iraqi will to resist the advance of coalition ground forces into Iraq and Kuwait.

Another justified element of the air war was interdiction of transport facilities between Baghdad and Basra. Destruction of an enemy's lines of communication weakens his ability to reinforce and resupply forces in the field, thus reducing the ability to defend against attacking forces on the ground.

Questions may be raised concerning the scope, duration and intensity of an air war which delivered more than 50,000 attacks and more than 88,500 tons of bombs against a clearly inferior foe. Nevertheless, to the extent that it satisfied legitimate requirements to get Iraqi forces out of Kuwait, they were justified within the scope of Resolution 678.

There are also two other factors which dictated the intense air war outside Kuwait. President Bush was very concerned, personally and politically, with minimizing US casualties in the ground war. Any action which contributed to that goal was fully justified in American eyes, no matter how much damage or destruction it caused in Iraq. Clearly there was also a US effort to minimize physical damage in Kuwait, which made attacks elsewhere more attractive to US targeteers.

Given all the arguments justifying the massive air assault on Iraq, it is nevertheless impossible to regard attacks directed against the Justice Ministry, Ba'ath Party facilities, and the Ministry of Municipal Affairs in Baghdad as directly, or indirectly, related to ousting Iraqi forces from Kuwait. Only by strained logic can water and power facilities in northern Iraq be related to reducing Iraqi military capabilities in Kuwait. Destruction of numerous industrial facilities throughout Iraq had little or nothing to do with implementing Resolution 678.

Taken all together, this far-reaching target list tends to show US intentions to gut the economic infrastructure of Iraq and at the same time to destroy the ability of the Saddam Hussein government to govern postwar Iraq. It also seems clear that one of the goals of Allied bombing was to make life in Iraq as difficult as possible in hopes of stimulating popular opposition to Saddam Hussein and thus bringing about his downfall.

The goal of rendering Iraq a political and economic nullity goes far beyond any UN resolution. In fact, it contravenes Resolution 674, which looks to possible reparations from Iraq. It will now be years before Iraq can restore its own economic health, let alone pay reparations.

There was more than a little irony in President Bush's statement on 13 March 1991 that he was concerned about the possibility that 'a vacuum in Iraq' might inhibit the development of stable political conditions in the Gulf region in the postwar period. He devoted a lot of American effort and money, even some lives, to creating that vacuum.

The other event which fairly raises a question about whether US objectives went beyond those of the UN occurred when Iraqi forces were attempting to leave Kuwait, beginning on 25 February. The question is: If the USA wanted only to implement the UN call for withdrawal, why were Iraqi troops attacked while they were leaving?

From the military viewpoint, once an adversary is engaged the battle must continue until he surrenders or is destroyed. Disengagement during a battle, particularly when one's own forces have the initiative, is unwise and risky. After all, the enemy may simply be withdrawing in order to set up new defences under more favourable conditions. Failure to prevent him from doing so could result in needless losses later.

That was clearly not the case on 25 February, however. From the very beginning of the coalition land offensive on 23 February, Iraqi forces had offered no organized or significant resistance. Coalition ground units were intended only to create a diversionary attack across the southern border of Kuwait on the 23rd. Meeting no resistance, however, they simply continued their northward advance unopposed. Brief resistance was experienced in the vicinity of the Kuwait International Airport, after which US units awaited the arrival of Kuwaiti forces to lead the triumphal entry into Kuwait City on 27 February.

Meanwhile, on the night of 25 February, Iraqi forces commenced what is referred to contemptuously as a 'bug out' from defensive positions in the city. It was these undisciplined, chaotic columns that were detected from the air and attacked ferociously for two days. Given that there had been no resistance to advancing coalition forces by Iraqi units in well-prepared defensive positions, it is unreasonable to conclude that the retreating hordes strung out along the road to Basra were effective forces bent upon setting up a new defence line in Kuwait.

The more logical conclusion is that US commanders had determined that it was no longer satisfactory for Iraqi forces to comply with Resolution 678 by withdrawing from Kuwait. The new objective was the destruction of as many Iraqi troops in Kuwait as possible. This objective was consistent with the conclusion above that the US air war exceeded UN objectives. All in all, it is clear that the US war aims were to destroy the economic, political and military strength of Iraq in order to render Iraq impotent in Middle Eastern affairs and to ensure the collapse of Saddam Hussein's government. No UN action ever authorized such goals.

## Appraising the Ground War

In the Gulf War the US and coalition military action on the ground was a brilliant success. Given the great imbalance of military power between Iraq and its opponents, the defeat of Iraq was preordained. It was not the sort of trial by fire that would permit us to characterize it as a great battle. Massive Iraqi surrenders reduced their level of resistance and the intensity of combat to virtual zero. The lack of Iraqi opposition resulted in a mercifully low coalition casualties. For this, everyone should be grateful. However, it must also be recognized that a great many postwar assessments about weapons performance and other measures of military effectiveness are not necessarily valid measures of combat potential in more demanding situations.

The lack of combat in this war is attributable to a number of factors. Much of the reason for the success was due to coalition commanders' prudent planning and willingness to give the air forces sufficient time to succeed on their own. The outcome was also due to Saddam Hussein's shortcomings as a military leader.

This may well have been the first war in history in which the air arm by itself was decisive in the victory. This decision in turn was achieved primarily by committing a very generous period of time to battlefield preparation. The air forces allied against Iraq flew nearly 110,000 sorties (about half of which were combat missions) and dropped 88,500 tons of munitions. About 7 per cent of the ordnance employed was more accurate than any used heretofore. Barring new revelations, the unrelenting bombardment probably did more than anything else to demoralize Iraqi soldiers everywhere in the theatre and crush their will to fight. The vast majority of the reported 100,000 Iraqi combat deaths were undoubtedly due to air attacks. While continuous bombing was surely not as accurate as it was portrayed on television, it is possible that the increased accuracy of precision-guided munitions contributed importantly to getting this job done.

No one can be sure, though, that the air war would have caused mass surrender of so many Iraqi troops had not the preparations for a ground offensive been so formidable. About 520,000 coalition ground troops were arrayed before the Iraqis, including the best-equipped, most mobile conventional forces in the world. This vast array represented more of a threat than numbers alone indicated. With unquestioned air supremacy and logistical muscle to support virtually unconstrained battlefield mobility, the view from Baghdad or Kuwait must have been terrifying indeed. To any military man the US forces clearly had the capability to sweep around either flank through seas of sand or water and to defeat any Iraqi attempt to blunt such moves.

The futility of the Iraqi predicament did not seem to have frightened Saddam Hussein. He blustered until the last days. However, there can be little doubt that Iraqi field commanders and many of the troops fully appreciated the lethality of the mechanized monster spread out before them. This, combined with the increasingly accurate hammering from the air, would explain most of the abject demoralization of the Iraqi defensive units. Extremely poor leadership on the part of Baghdad's political leaders and military officers also contributed to the loss of will to fight.

Some observers might ask, in view of the unexpected rapidity of the coalition ground forces' victory, whether the huge troop deployment was overkill. Even in hindsight, however, it seems prudent and sensible for General Schwarzkopf to have planned his attack on the assumption that Iraqi resistance would be greater on the ground than during any other phase of the war. The precise degree of force needed in war is always hard to predict. It is especially difficult to estimate how much shock action it will take to achieve a breakthrough against well-prepared defences. Other intangibles, like panic and mass capitulation, are impossible to predict.

Furthermore, the American leadership was understandably gun-shy about underestimating a Third World foe, no matter how inept that enemy appeared, in view of their protracted mistakes with the Vietnamese from 1965 to 1973. The American generals in the Persian Gulf were not about to escalate incrementally, nor to hold back any coercive measures at their disposal. The last thing anyone might expect from the US military in this war was a low estimate of the force required.

The sudden collapse of Iraqi army resistance loses most of its mystery when the poor decisions made by Saddam Hussein and his officers are factored into the equation. He undermined any likeli-hood of military gains by choosing in the first place to confront a superpower in a classic setpiece engagement. That decision alone maximized most of the USA's high-technology advantages and reduced whatever advantages might have accrued to an experienced army defending its homeland. In addition, he worsened his own cause by bunching up his numerically superior army in a geographi-cally confined space where it could easily be surrounded and cut off.

The final blow to his own cause was stunning in that Saddam Hussein let his troops know there was no need to defend to the end. His last-minute offer to the Soviets to withdraw from Kuwait may have been a desirable diplomatic move, but it was a serious blunder militarily. A 'will to fight' is one of those intangibles crucial to military success. Saddam Hussein's announcement that he was willing to give up Iraqi claims to Kuwait put an end to any remaining will to fight among his troops in Kuwait.

In the final analysis, it was a combination of overwhelming US military force and Iraqi ineptitude that were the prime elements in the victory. Reliable conclusions and lessons must be based upon a careful examination of what can and cannot be legitimately derived from this seven-month experience. Most air-delivered weapons systems were battle-tested against Iraq, while the great majority of ground systems were not.

The most important revelations of this great offensive operation turn out to be unexpected. One of the most interesting is that even large-scale conventional regional wars can be fought from bases in the continental USA. The so-called 'forward deployment' of American forces to such places as Europe, Japan and Korea made only minor contributions to the success of Desert Storm. Troops that were shipped to Saudi Arabia from Europe could have been shipped more readily from the USA. In the USA units would have had contingency plans for all varieties of air, land and sea shipment from numerous points of embarkation. This was not the case for forward-deployed units in Europe. They planned the move to the Persian Gulf nearly from scratch and executed it no faster than any of the divisions deployed originally from the USA. Some political problems as well were faced in moving forces from Europe to the Middle East.

Since the collapse of the Warsaw Pact in 1989, the Pentagon has consistently maintained that so-called 'regional wars' are the primary military threat that our forces must face. If forward deployment contributed so little to this first large post-Cold War regional conflict, perhaps serious scrutiny is warranted of the billions currently spent on forward-deployed armed forces.

Still more unexpected is the negative conclusion one must draw about the viability of future military intervention as a tool of US foreign policy. Ironically, Desert Storm may have marked the end, not the beginning, of large-scale conventional warfare in distant regions of the globe. While there will probably be future regional wars, few indeed will be conventional in nature. After the disastrous defeat suffered by Iraq, widely labelled as one of the top four armies in the world, who will risk a conventional armed confrontation with the USA in the future? The number of cross-border regional wars of the conventional variety will probably drop dramatically. The Pentagon has maintained for some time that insurgency and guerrilla fighting, under the military rubric of Low-Intensity Conflict (LIC), would be the most likely of all wars in the future. This starkly one-sided example of high-intensity operations by a major military power in the Gulf War makes this long-held expectation more likely to come true.

Neither the US government nor the military have anything to learn about guerrilla warfare from the Desert Storm experience. Rather than encourage future interventions by its success, the war with Iraq should be recognized by the public as an example of what is least likely to recur. Future resort to forceful intervention could be a nasty experience, like Vietnam, in which almost none of the lessons of Desert Storm will apply.

The military have every right to be proud of the ground forces' performance, and Americans can be thankful that the land combat succeeded decisively at very little cost in American lives. But the public, as well as the policy-makers, in the USA should also remain very cautious about drawing too many long-term conclusions from America's desert war.

## Exorcizing the Vietnam Syndrome?

Perceptions of America's war with Vietnam had a great deal to do with the shape of the recent war in the Middle East. So-called lessons from Vietnam were applied, with devastating impact on Iraq. Today's US military leaders are heavily influenced by their selective views of the Vietnam experience. American politicians and the American public have also shared attitudes towards the use of military power that were extremely influential in shaping the US approach to the confrontation with Iraq.

The notion that if war comes it should be fought with little restraint, employing overwhelming military power to achieve rapid victory, is the chief 'lesson' that the American military have derived from the Vietnam War. The heightened role of airpower and bombing in such a military success was stressed by Secretary of Defense James Schlesinger in 1975: 'One of the lessons of the Vietnamese conflict is that rather than simply counter your opponent's thrusts, it is necessary to go for the heart of the opponent's power. Destroy his military forces rather than simply being involved endlessly in ancillary military operations.' Despite the fact that more explosive tonnage was dropped by US warplanes over Indochina than was dropped in World War II and Korea combined, this odd notion that American military 'restraint' was the chief problem in the Vietnam War has become an unquestioned axiom.

The singular importance of minimizing American casualties so as to retain public support for war is another lesson for both American military and political officials. The sophisticated management and control of press coverage of war, and preparation for war, has also been highly refined since the Vietnam era.

Contrary to impressions of American preoccupation with the legacy of Vietnam over the past fifteen years, the fact is that there was little thoughtful evaluation of the larger political and military meaning of the Vietnam conflict on the part of the American establishment. As soon as that war ended, the Executive branch pushed to loosen Congressional and public-opinion restraints on the government's power of intervention and freedom of action abroad. Those who raised doubts were labelled 'isolationists'. The call was for the American people to be reawakened to the 'realities of power' and their 'responsibilities' around the world.

American foreign policy since 1975 has often repeated many of the errors of the Vietnam period: inadequate use of political and diplomatic means; premature resort to force; reluctant consultation with Congress; acting on incomplete and faulty information; exaggerated self-serving rhetoric; and too much concern for 'image'. The US confrontation with Iraq showed all the hallmarks of these faults.

In 1984 Defense Secretary Caspar Weinberger propounded six major tests to be applied when the USA is considering the use of combat forces abroad:

1. The United States should not commit forces to combat overseas unless the particular engagement or occasion is deemed vital to our national interest or that of our allies.

2. If we decide it is necessary to put combat troops into a given situation, we should do so wholeheartedly, and with the clear intention of winning.

3. If we do decide to commit forces to combat overseas, we should have clearly defined political and military objectives. And we should know precisely how our forces can accomplish those clearly defined objectives. And we should have and send the forces needed to do just that.

4. The relationship between our objectives and the forces we have committed ... must be continually reassessed and adjusted if necessary.

5. Before the USA commits combat forces abroad, there must be some reasonable assurance we will have the support of the American people and their elected representatives in Congress.

6. The commitment of US forces to combat should be a last resort.

Whether the US approach to the recent war in the Middle East met all these criteria is debatable. Certainly the injunction to do whatever is necessary to win was followed rigorously. Before the war started in January 1991, however, many Americans, including nearly half of the members of Congress and many senior retired National Security officials, argued that the USA had not exhausted non-military means at its disposal.

The UN-endorsed goal of getting the Iraqis out of Kuwait provided a clearly defined military objective. The larger Bush Administration goal of affecting major political and military changes within Iraq has been much less clearly defined, and it is far from certain that these changes will be in the real interests of the USA and other countries in the region.

American euphoria about the military victory over Iraq will probably fuel the well-ingrained propensity to act as the world's police. That habit, born of the Cold War and given full expression in Vietnam, has now been given a new lease of life in the post-Cold War world.

The authors wish to acknowledge the assistance of Center for Defense Information staff David Isenberg, David Johnson and Piers Wood.

# GRACE PALEY

## Something about the Peace Movement: Something about the People's Right Not to Know

One Saturday in late March 1991: the Gulf War has ended. The Iraqis, retreating, have been bombed and strafed on their road home, having unwisely turned their backs to us. The war is not over.

I am walking with my women friends. They are a group that calls itself WIMPS: Women Indict Military Policies. They're a part of the Peace Movement that thinks about peace even when the newspapers say there's no war. We're walking single file, led by a solemn drum beat through the streets of our neighbourhood in lower Manhattan. Our postwar signs say IS THE MIDDLE EAST MORE STABLE NOW? One sign has a picture of an Iraqi child. Across his chest the words *Collateral Damage* are superimposed.

We're surprised when people thank us for our flyers and for our presence in the streets. Every now and then some old-fashioned person says 'Go back to Russia'. Or a modern fellow says 'Go kiss Saddam's ass'. But we're in New York, where the yellow ribbons that have tied our country into a frightened sentimental knot are not so prevalent.

I've been in the US Peace or Anti-War Movement since before the Vietnam War, the mid 1950s. In fact that war interrupted the work many people were doing in trying to end militarism, and prevent nuclear war and nuclear proliferation.

In 1961 I was invited to join a group called the Greenwich Village Peace Center, founded by the American Friends Service Committee which with its customary wisdom left us alone to figure

**61**

out concensus, non-violence decentralized or direct action. We had come from neighbourhood concerns: schools, parks, transport. Many of us had children and were worried about the nuclear tests that were sending radioactivity into the air – particularly Strontium 90, which travelled through air, to grass, to cows, to our children's milk. We didn't like the arms race which, during air-raid drills, forced our children to hide under school desks. We were not so much understanding as experiencing the connections. We had, I suppose, been scratching around furiously under the oppression of McCarthyism and were glad to have come together in an autonomous way that was also sensible and communal.

One day our friend and board member Dr Otto Nathan[1] said, 'You know, there is the beginning of a war in South-East Asia in a country, very small, called Vietnam. We are now in there with advisers – all kinds of soldiers, soon – who knows? – we have to pay attention.'

We *did* pay attention a couple of weeks later by holding a meeting and discussion (not called a teach-in yet). Just an educational event at a local church, well attended – and then our slow work began as the war itself slowly gathered its political and military determination to slaughter a million Vietnamese as well as 58,000 Americans.

Now I will tell you something about the ways we organized against this war – how roughly 3,500 events were successfully hidden from other Americans and the world; how it was shaken by the terrible accumulating speed of the Gulf War. It's as though the war itself were one of those smart weapons, the market systems directed trajectories tested in vicious electoral campaigns and used in this case to eliminate the Peace Movement and its national and historical accomplishment, the Vietnam Syndrome. At this moment of triumph, with 300 Americans and 100,000 Iraquis dead, the President announced that he had indeed extinguished the Peace Movement and ended the Vietnam Syndrome. Was the main purpose of the Gulf War to bathe the American conscience in blood so as to give it a taste for blood? Well, certainly that was one of its purposes.

The Peace Movement itself is a valuable old fact, unstable at its broadest constituency, rock solid at its centre. It lives, as many readers know – broad or narrow – in our rich, powerful, somewhat backward, secretly poor, racist, uncomfortably large democratic nation, the United States – which is also cranky and righteous. The elections every four years are considered the final responsibility of citizenship, though usually only about 50 per cent of registered voters vote. That's why it takes an awful lot of time and nerve for people to speak up. (That's why a short war is best.) If, on a street corner while giving out flyers, you ask someone why they don't speak up, they are apt to say they don't need to; we're already a democracy. Our two political parties, smiling proudly at one another, enable us to demand lots of pluralism in other countries.[2]

Now how should I describe how this war's peace movement happened? There were already women and men innocently joyful about the end of the Cold War (me too), believing we'd come to that moment in our lifetimes when serious internal expensive problems could be addressed. The Panama invasion was a bad sign, but if you work in any oppositional movement you will be opposed vigorously. (This surprises some people.) We didn't expect things to be easy, but we had added hope to the personality, if not the character, of our work. The continuing anti-war workers were doing the usual anti-militarism work – against the arms budget (much of it hidden in costs of old wars, hidden too in the Energy Department budget), the fight against underground testing, classes in non-violence, anti-recruitment drives in high schools. And a boycott of war toys. It seemed clearer with each Administration decision that President Bush and his warrior companions had drawn their first line of sand in the sandbox in a tough school, and they hadn't changed too much – in action or in boy language.

Environmental organizations were doing their important work globally and in village toxic dumps. The Central American networks were dealing with decades of exported US repression and war. Feminist groups – radical, socialist, academic or traditional – were facing backlashes that often follow success – the anti-abortion moralities of the anti-sexual right as well as the wishful pronouncements of patriarchy that feminism was dead. Blacks and other people of colour also hoped that the inner-city disasters of homelessness and poverty would be reversed somehow, although racism, as the most severe inherited illness of the United States, was continuing its nasty life. Gay groups struggled with discrimination and the grief of Aids. Middle Eastern organizations suffered indifference and faced nearly everyone else's ignorance . . . at a time when their role was about to become central.

I've told you all this to show that radical and social justice organizations had plenty to do. But the experience of Vietnam and the work of decades began to pay off. In general most of the groups I've described saw their connections to one another – were in fact living those connections. Before the coalition (two in some places – three in Seattle, I've been told – at first anyway) there was a lot of overlapping. For instance, many women in Central American work were feminists. They listened to the radio and watched television and heard the drone and confidence of pro-war male experts – even more tedious than some of their political brothers. It's hard to believe that fifteen years ago, people opposed to nuclear power and anti-nuclear-war activists didn't understand that they had a common agenda. It took long discussions and a couple of years of political argument and mediation to bring them together. Environmentalists had to learn that war made an ecological mess. Oh? First resistance. Then surprise. Then connection.

On 29 August 1990 Jeff Patterson refused to join his unit; he sat down on the airstrip in Hawaii. He had enlisted in the Marine Corps straight out of high school in California – for the same reason most youngsters do: educational opportunities, maybe some adventure. His experience during deployments to Okinawa, South Korea and the Philippines changed his outlook entirely. He said, 'I have, as an artillery controller, directed cannons on Oahu, rained burning white phosphorus and tons of high explosives on the big island and blasted away at the island of Kahoolawe . . . I can bend no further.' In the next few weeks, others were to join him.

On 12 September 1990 one of the first peace meetings in New York was held at Cooper Union. There were thousands of women and men – the auditorium was full; there were loudspeakers outside. The weather was fine and the plaza around Cooper Union packed with intent listeners. I have been living in white Vermont, and as a true New Yorker I became excited to see once again all the colours of the people of my city. And the numbers! A surprise really. Oh, I thought – this war will never happen.

At the literature table I looked at various flyers and petitions, particularly the flyer and petition issued by the coalition that had put this marvellous meeting together with its twenty to thirty speakers. I thought it was all right – kind of jargony, but not too terrible. This huge meeting was what mattered.

Still, I did say to the young woman at the lit table: 'How come you guys left out the fact that Iraq did go into Kuwait? How come?' She said, 'That's not really important.' 'I know what you mean,' I said, 'but it happens to be true.'

I did know what she meant and I read their explanation a couple of weeks later. It insisted that if the American people were told about the invasion of Kuwait, they would 'become confused'. It would 'obfuscate' the basic facts and actions. Unfortunately, of course, the American people had already been told and continued to be told day and night about this pathetic little country of trillionaires, and so omitting facts became a kind of lie and did get in the way of organizing people unaccustomed to being held to political lines. It was a stubbornness that hurt work in New York more than elsewhere, but people are used to that, and national – I should say local – organizing all around the country against the frighteningly speedy troop and propaganda build-up continued. Reports of their success vary according to the facts and the disposition of the reporter.

Two coalitions finally had to happen in New York. One was the Coalition to Stop Intervention in the Middle East, which, with its strong cadre of the Workers' World Party, had organized the important New York 12 September meeting; the other became the National Campaign for Peace in the Middle East, with its base in traditional peace and anti-intervention groups. The division was real, a matter of substance, style – and at the same time there were organizations that had simply started to do their anti-Gulf War in one coalition or another – also it depended on how much they were doing outside the big cities. An example would be Palestinian Aid in the Coalition and Palestinian Solidarity in the Campaign. The division came to a pointy head over the dates of the major Washington demonstration. The Coalition had decided on the 19th before a common meeting with the Campaign. Reasons for both were as good as they were bad. It was good to do it on Martin Luther King's holidays weekend, because . . . Yes, I thought. It was bad to plan it for that weekend, because . . . Yes, I thought. In any event, the vote ran extremely high against the 19th.

In late December 1990 the Campaign proposed a joint statement supporting both demonstrations. The Coalition said No. Many people went to both. The Coalition went ahead, had its demonstration on the 19th with good representation of people of colour, Blacks, Hispanics, many Middle Eastern Americans. In San Francisco there were about 150,000 demonstrators. The 26th brought out about 250,000 people in Washington. The tone, the style of these demonstrations were extraordinary. There were more hand-made, non-organizational signs as well as the big ballooning sky-hiding world hoisted above us all by Greenpeace. The Bread and Puppet marched with its huge puppets, its great music and stilt dancers and its Vermont Cadre of a couple of hundred B and P lovers and activist banner-carriers. Some of the signs – culled from my head and *The Nation*: WAR IS GOOD BUSINESS; INVEST YOUR SON OR DAUGHTER; GEORGE BUSH IS HAVING A WARGASM; A KINDER GENTLER BLOODBATH; GIVE OESTROGEN A CHANCE; READ MY APOCALYPSE.

These impressive demonstrations happened later, after the war had started but before the rage and drive of the air war and its murderous pre-emption of hope taught us to say the word 'blitz-krieg' and understand where our civilian and military leaders had gone to school.

I want to say a little more about the opposition to the inevitable war before 15 January 1991. Interesting fact: 73 per cent of American women were opposed to the war in the month before it started. Men were split down the middle.

The *New York Times* printed a letter on 22 August 1990 from Alex Molnar whose son, a twenty-one-year-old Marine, had been sent to Saudi Arabia. He concluded his letter (to President Bush): 'And I'm afraid that as the pressure mounts, you will wager my son's life in a gamble to save your political future . . .' The letter was reprinted many times and created a movement called the Military Families Support Network . . . which by early March 1991 had chapters in thirty-nine states. MFSN supported the use of economic sanctions, opposed massive deployment of US forces and the entire military offensive. Their emphasis on the support of troops has put off a number of columnists. I myself feel that a slogan like Support the Troops has to include the words By Bringing Them Home Now.

Actually, in almost every demonstration I've been a part of or come upon in another city or town, those last words *were* there. There's a kind of critiquing of the events and actions of that hard short period that is not criticism but more like an academic exercise made by people at their desks who are not out on the streets or engaged in the decision-making processes of any non-centralized organization.

Journeys, peace missions to Iraq or journeys of inquiry have been a part of peace movement activity from late summer/early autumn 1991, when they began organizing, into February 1991 and the war.

In mid October a peace delegation organized by the Fellowship of Reconciliation spent two days in Jordan and a week in Iraq. The main purpose of this mission was to bring medicines to Amman and especially to Baghdad. David McReynolds, one of the members of the twenty-person team, returned and reported on the lives of children in Baghdad. I think of one scene he describes: fathers in a small Iraqi village holding their children up to the windows of the Americans bus. I did not see this report in our newspapers.

The Gulf Peace Team opened a Peace Camp on the border of Iraq and Saudi Arabia. It remained there for ten days and thousands of sorties of the air war. It was evacuated on 26 January 1991 by the Iraqis. There were eighty-six witnesses living at the camp, many from other countries as well as the United States. They saw the beginning of the environmental destruction by our smart air force and the great suffering of the people. I read their reports in the left and pacifist press.

Later – in early February, during the war – Ramsey Clark and a group of well-known photographers and reporters went, including an American Iraqi with family there who was able to bring him into conversation with ordinary civilians and their experiences – beginning with the bombed road from Jordan into Iraq and the destruction of civilian vehicles – food and grain trucks. Also the markets, water stations, schools – all the targets, I guess, of our 'stupid' bombs.

To return to prewar actions, statements . . . On 14 November the National Council of Churches at a conference in Portland, Oregon condemned US policy in the Gulf: 'As Christians . . . we must witness against weak resignation to the illogical logic of militarism and war.' The National Conference of Catholic Bishops wrote to President Bush: 'in this situation, moving beyond the deployment of military forces in an effort to deter Iraq's aggression to the undertaking of offensive military action could well violate the criteria for a "just war", especially the principles of proportionality and last resort.'

These strong leadership statements stood, but the churches themselves fell into an awful quietness as the war began. I am reminded here that it's important to say that the religious Fellowships, the Catholic and Jewish, the Protestant Peace churches as well, did *not* retreat. What happened to churches and congregations sincerely opposed to the war to begin with is what happened to Congressmen and Senators who swore they'd never back down. The sight of a yellow ribbon unnerved them. They fell before it, just as tyrants and Satans had once fallen before the cross placed before their terrified eyes.

Meanwhile, in the rest of the country, hundreds of meetings, vigils, sit-ins, teach-ins, were occurring. By early March 1991 over 3,500 actions had happened and over 4,000 arrests had been made. In our valley (between New Hampshire and Vermont) perhaps a dozen small towns held regular vigils. A newspaper advertisement was signed by 1,100 people. Who were they? The women and men who drove in and out of dirt roads were probably 1960s folks, now forty or so, with kids – or not – also Vietnam Vets. But the signers were often old budget enemies from town meetings, people seen only at the dump or recycling centre – or in church. We were amazed – What? She signed! That one! But this was before the war ... Vigils continued through the weeks of the war. We are going back now to the signers. What will we find?

Full-page advertisements were taken out by SaneeFreeze and the Ad Hoc Committee which also organized teach-ins. Communications from other parts of the country tell the same story – sometimes more original. Seven or eight men and women from Oakland travelled the train system singing funny anti-Bush lyrics. They were applauded and cursed. Here are some quotes from Lucy Lippard's report in *Z* of artists and just plain creative people's responses to the prospects of war and to the war itself.

Our street theater piece 'The Bushs Take You For A Ride' has George and Barbara in a red cardboard car running out of gas and being 'serviced' by a soldier/gas pump – GI Jose. A hose from his red satin heart is administered by a 'Plasmaco nursery' representing Petroleum Multinational. When the soldier collapses, the audience is solicited for more volunteers.

Two of Boulder's most effective cultural groups are satirical. LISP (Ladies in Support of the President) is 'an organization of patriotic God-fearing LADIES who deplore nasty war protests' and offer 'George is not a Wimp' buttons. An offshoot of the local Queer Cosmos, these men in drag haunt recruitment centers and plead prissily at rallies for 'all you homosexuals and commies to please go home.' A long standing socialist feminist group (with anti-racist 'Klarette' performances and a public 'Sodomy Patrol' among their past credits) are polling crowds.

GRIT (Gulf Response Information Team, 'a very private research group') are sending the results to the President. Their questions begin straight, sucking people in, and end with outrageous ones, like 'In order to support our troops, how many casualties from your family would be acceptable? (a) 1 (b) 2 (c) 3 or more (d) all of them.'

Small groups like GRIT, and individual artists, can be less intimidating and attract less hostility and more dialogue than massive demonstrations, which serve another purpose. For instance, playwright Art Mayers patrolled Augusta, Maine's state capitol, in Arab headdress and gas mask dripping blood, muttering over and over, 'the horror of it, the horror of it.' He was eventually arrested for 'terrorizing children,' but the charges were dropped.

When I stopped at the office of the War Resisters' League to pick up some flyers, they were receiving as many as ninety calls a day asking for military counselling, from reservists as well as active-duty men *and* women. A high-school kid who's just enlisted was speaking to Peter Jamieson, a Vietnam Vet (he's a counsellor). Michael Marsh, who has organized the work in this office, is down at Camp LeJeune, North Carolina, where seven Marine COs are being court-martialled on charges of desertion. I was given a sheet of paper listing fifteen resisters. In Germany there are American soldiers at US bases who are resisting deployment. A Military Counselling Network has been in place since early autumn – AFSC, WRL and CCCO were major networkers.

A fine project which, with more money could have got under way earlier, was Madre's tour of Women of Courage. Madre, whose major political work had been about Nicaragua, especially the women, their hospitals and daycare centres, had undertaken to send about twenty women from different Middle Eastern countries on tour through the United States and Canada. While one group spoke in New England, others were in Toronto – and in Californian cities. Women from Iraq, Turkey, Palestine, Egypt and Israel were in the group I heard. Each city or two visited had to add an American mother whose son or daughter was in the desert.

In going over material I'd gathered for this chapter, I found something I'd written to a friend I work and think with at the very beginning of January 1991:

Another thing I worry about: Resistance to this war is great. So – if we *do* go to war, it will take a lot of hard-working repression to keep that anger in check or turn it around. We better watch out for it. It will only *start* with the suppression of information from the front and continue by hiding our regional and town actions from one another till we think we or our villages or our families are alone.

This is exactly what happened: the pools. According to the Fund for Free Expression, of the 1,400 journalists in the Persian Gulf only 192 – including technicians and photographers – were placed in press pools with combat forces. Journalists 'apprehended or threatened with detention or detained include E. Schmitt and Kifner of the *New York Times*, Gughliotti of the *Washington Post*, King and Bayles of the Associated Press . . . These are people who did try to break free of government censors . . .' 'A French TV crew was forced at gunpoint by US marines to give up videotape it had shot of US wounded in the battle to retake the Saudi town of Khafji.'

Almost overnight, once the war started, the silence began. Having lived for sixty-eight years, a surprising number of them in some political consciousness, I must report that I've never experienced the kind of repression that set in once the air war started. It was not like the McCarthy period – that is there were no personal direct attacks on well-known people of that kind. It was as though a great damp blanket had been laid over our country with little pinholes for American flags to stick up into the public air.

Here is another paragraph from the 27 February 1991 report of the Fund for Free Expression:

There have been several instances of retaliation against journalists who have questioned the propriety of the war. After he wrote approvingly of an antiwar march, *San Francisco Examiner* associate editor and columnist Warren Hinckle was put on a partially paid three-month leave. 'I take the position that I was censored,' Hinckle says. The editor of the Kutztown, Pennsylvania *Patriot* was fired after he wrote an editorial calling for peace. *Village Voice* national affairs editor Dan Bischoff was canceled as a guest on the CBS news 'Nightwatch' program. The Pentagon refused to provide anyone to appear on the program if the *Voice* was to be represented among the participants. The program's producer recalls a Pentagon representative as objecting on the grounds that 'if someone from *The Village Voice* is on, that raises the possibility that there will be a discussion of the merits' of the lawsuit filed by the *Voice* and other media organizations challenging the Pentagon press restrictions. The Public Broadcasting System postponed a rebroadcast of a Bill Moyers 'Frontline' program on the Iran–Contra affair because, according to an internal PBS memo, the program's raising of 'serious questions about then-Vice

President Bush's involvement and actions' make it 'journalistically inappropriate' during the war against Iraq, because 'the program could be viewed as overtly political by attempting to undermine the President's credibility.'

FAIR – Fairness and Accuracy in Reporting – offered the following report on 22 February:

> About 1.5 per cent of nightly news programs . . . were identified as anti-war protests. Only one leader of a peace organization was quoted in broadcasts surveyed. Seven Super Bowl players were sought out to comment on the war. Half of all sources were connected to US or Allied governments, 3 in 10 from the military.

Another report on television – this time by three academic researchers, Sut Jhally, Justin Lewis and Michael Morgan, learnt that there was a correlation between knowledge – information – and opposition to the war. Television viewing was broken down into three groups. The longer people looked at television – the less they knew. The short-time viewers were not well informed, but much better informed than the others. After some of these protests which followed FAIR's exposés, certain programmes like the MacNeil Lehrer Hour (daily) finally allowed Noam Chomsky, Erwin Knoll and Edward Said to speak their dissenting views.

It's not as though media workers on our side didn't fight back. Paper Tiger/Deep Dish produced a Gulf Crisis TV series – seen on Public Access channels and finally PBS (Public Broadcasting). Tapes were used in university teach-ins.


When Peace People (organizers) talked critically of the period, they varied – widely. Frances Crowe, in Western Massachusetts, 'found a huge anti-war movement waiting to be organized. After ten years of trying to organize around the Middle East, people are ready and willing to learn about the region.' Susan Akram asks, 'How did the Peace Movement get so isolated?'

I've tried to describe in these few pages something about what has been happening in the last months in my country. I've left out a lot – by necessity.

If you were part of these events, if you were working in your community, you had a sense of excitement, action, momentum, but at the same time, listening to radio, television news, or reading the daily press, darkened you into an unimaginable despair. Not only the sense of a vast damp blanket over the country, but also it seemed that half your neighbours not only didn't know, but *wanted not to know* because if a bit of news squeaked through (the bombing of the Baghdad shelter) there were cries of 'Treason!' (the photographers, the anchor men, the television station).

One of the responses to this war that grieved me particularly was the failure of American Jews to see how bad this war was for Israel, how dangerous, how destructive it *had* to be for the hopes for peace and a decent relationship with Palestinians – how it set all that struggle back years and years.

So the war ends – and doesn't end. It never ended for the Vietnamese – all these embargoed years. Not for the Panamanians either, who are worse off than ever. Not for the Middle East, where as I write, hundreds of thousands of Kurds running, fighting, encouraged by Bush's rhetoric of rebellion, are being slaughtered by Iraq's helicopters and starved and frozen in their tracks. Hundreds of thousands of Iraqis dead, injured, leave the countryside and the destroyed cities in grief and turmoil. We've learnt that *only 7 per cent* of our thousands of sorties were so-called smart bombs. The rest were the usual stupid carpet bombs, cluster bombs, etc., used for civilians, ground armies, the earth . . .

Israelis and Palestinians hate each other more than ever – both people having been driven mad: the Israelis by Europeans fifty years ago; the Palestinians by Israelis today. The Palestinians running from the country Kuwait, that we liberated so that it could continue along its glowing golden road. The oppression of Palestinians in the occupied territories is worse than ever, partly because they made the wrong (foolish) decision to agree with Saddam Hussein, partly because Israel was planning to make it tougher to be a Palestinian anyway.

Why were Bush and friends so determined to jam this war down the originally disinterested throats of Allies – the UN and US – the American citizenry. We learnt – little by little. First everyone said Oil! Of course. Then we learnt that we used very little of Kuwait's oil. So we understood next it was about hegemony – that is, being in charge of everyone else's oil. A major purpose was the great Pentagon need to try out all the new so far unused trillion dollars' worth of airware. How would they perform? Many years ago, in 1969, a North Vietnamese said to me as I was leaving Hanoi, 'Please tell the great American scientists to stop using us as their laboratory. Your napalm *does* work. So does your improved white phosphorus.' Our government also wanted to teach an important lesson: it was possible to move over 400,000 troops in a few weeks halfway round the fattest part of the earth.

It was also a major necessity to wipe out the historical memory of the 1960s, which moved more powerfully than is usually perceived into the 1970s with the rise of the women's movement, the anti-nuclear power movement and the science of ecology with its working arm, environmentalism.

I am reminded of a statement made by Donella Meadows at a Dartmouth teach-in. She explained that there was alternative energy for everything in normal comfortable American life – television, air conditioners, light, heat, cars. There was only one enterprise that required such massive infusion of energy for which no alternative to oil could work – and that was war. A tank, she said, could move only 17 feet on a gallon of petrol. So this is the final purpose. This has been a war to maintain turmoil in the world (particularly in the Middle East). This has been a war to ensure that Americans can continue to make war, and like it.

## Notes

1. Dr Otto Nathan, Einstein's executor, an economist, said sadly to me one day, 'You know, it isn't guns *or* butter. If THEY wanted it, the country could have guns *and* butter.' When I mentioned this to other smart economists, they disagreed. The thirty years of simple American malice since then have inclined me to agree with Dr Nathan.

2. Vermont, where I now live, elected an independent socialist, a terrible shock to the US Congress.

# DR FADIA FAQIR

## Tales of War: Arab Women in the Eye of the Storm[1]

> Who makes history? Us or him? The World Order wants to renew himself and draws himself the future image of the sun, the moon, and other planets and the ants which live on them . . . Who makes history? Us or them? Those who walk on green grass or those who pollute earth and space with atomic waste? Producers of the war machine or its defenceless opponents?
>
> *Zulaykha Abu-Risha, Jordanian woman writer*[2]

There is no peace in the Arab house – the domestic world of most Arab women. They continue their daily work, trying to keep the household together, while waiting for their husbands and sons to return from the front line or the chambers of the secret police. They suffer bereavement in silence.[3] Women strive to keep the morale of the family high, to stabilize the home, as war follows war. Regimes that Arab women never voted for[4] or supported take whole nations to war, destroying generation after generation. Through their windows women watch, bewildered, as the funeral procession passes, the coffins streaming down the street. Having no say in what takes place in the political arena, they, together with their children, are the forgotten casualties of the cycles of violence.

### Palestine and Lebanon

When this war started, the sad eyes of Huria and Fadi followed me round the house. Huria Houran, the thin, pale Palestinian teacher of English in Ain el-Helweh[5] Camp near Sidon, Lebanon, who always starts her lesson, whether it is on the passive voice or the present continuous, with the following question: 'Who is missing today?' And Fadi, the five-year-old Lebanese boy who, unable to take any more of the sound of bombardment,[6] shut himself in the refrigerator. My Lebanese women friends always talk about the 'Lebanese disease' – the physical and mental exhaustion which then develops into a severe migraine. When they go to the doctor, he tells them there is nothing wrong with them except the fact that they are Lebanese, and bereavement and loss are things they must get used to. That 'Lebanese disease' is no longer unique to Lebanon and the Lebanese: it has spread to Iraq and Kuwait to plague the heads and hearts of women there. That disease first broke out in Palestine, where it all started . . .

'God bless you, my daughter, you are right. It all started in Palestine,' said Umm-Khalid,[7] and smiled. Her face is old and wrinkled, but used to smiling. Her white veil is pinned tightly under her chin, covering her grey plaits. She straightened her long, black skirt, and said, 'I am from Nablus, the West Bank. I have a large family and we've been living in a refugee camp for the last twenty years. My young ones are at home; the military governor has shut down the schools and universities – he wants my children to remain illiterate, like me. They've got used to the tear gas and the banging on doors. The soldiers come at night to search our houses and arrest our sons. Three years ago they took Walid, my nineteen-year-old son, and put him in prison.[8] The Israeli authorities accused him of working for the leadership of the *intifada*. Every Friday, I visit him in Junaid prison and take him some food. Sometimes the authorities don't let us in, so I stand with the other mothers outside the prison gate and shout, "Walid, how are you? I'm here! Don't despair, we are with you!"

'When the war in the Gulf started, they put us under curfew. We have been under curfew for many months now. The whole family has to stay in this shack. My youngest, Moona, has begun crying for no reason at all. They let us out of our houses for three hours a day to buy food. But we have no money to buy anything. We might as well stay imprisoned in our houses. Arab workers are not allowed to cross the Green Line any more, not allowed to build their villas for them.[9] So Abu-Khalid, my ageing husband, has been sitting here since this war started. I use the three hours they give me on Fridays to visit Walid in prison.

'How can I travel to Kuwait to visit my eldest son Khalid? I don't know. God bless him, he used to work in Kuwait[10] and send me some money at the beginning of every month. They say he lost his job when the war started. One of our relatives told me that he is in prison in Kuwait.[11] They are torturing him, just as the Israelis tortured his brother Walid. Who visits him? Who brings him food? I wish I could cross the river to see him. I have never left Nablus since we arrived in 1967. I do not even known how to cross. They say I don't have the right card and papers . . .'

Umm-Khalid's dwindling voice echoes in my head. My displaced Palestinian son, Haitham, talks about Jaffa as if he had been born there: the port, the old streets, and the mosque. He talks about his grandparents' exodus from Palestine as if he was the baby whose cot had been hidden from Israeli jets under trees, not his father. And now, after the war, he talks of Scuds, jet-fighter bombers, and victory – 'Victory is sweet with the help of Allah,' said Saddam Hussein. What kind of future will we leave Haitham and all other Arab children? An occupied Palestine, a destroyed Kuwait and Iraq, and a Middle East polluted by smoke and hatred. Is that our legacy to the future generations in the Arab world? His eyes, too, follow me round the house. Since the war, I cannot shake off this clinging sense of guilt . . .

## Kuwait

A reign of terror began in your country on the 2nd of August. For your house to be searched became a daily occurrence. For your husband and sons to be taken at gunpoint became part of your life. Your young children started wetting their beds and developed a stutter. You could not inquire about the members of your family who disappeared for fear of being arrested yourself. You had to help families forced to evacuate their houses, to help them settle in and provide food for them all somehow. So soon you learnt how to hide the men, and to dress the wounds of those who were taken and tortured . . .

'I have just arrived from Kuwait,' said Umm-Ramadan.[12] She is a sturdy woman and she covers her head with a white scarf; her baby daughter is wrapped in her black *abaya*. 'I live in al-Surra, in Kuwait City. On Friday night, after the evening prayers, I washed my face and went again to al-Surra police station to ask about Ramadan, my eighteen-year-old son, who was arrested by the Iraqi soldiers. They accused me of distributing leaflets for the Resistance. They told me he was not there. Ten days later he was released and I went to collect him from al-Farwaniyya police station. When I saw his face, I could not control my tears. In ten days they had added ten years to his life. His ears and lips were swollen where they had applied electricity. I held his hand and walked him out under the smoky sky of Kuwait. He could not speak or walk normally. Leaning on me, panting, he walked into our house. I put him to bed and tried to feed him some soup. He shook his head and went to sleep . . .'

What kind of evil has plagued Kuwait? An old evil that has practised and perfected its methods on its own subjects.[13] An evil that has been roaming the streets of Arab countries for decades. I think of my friend Hassan, who was taken to prison for leafleting: a well-built twenty-one-year old engineer, with dark hair and kind eyes. Nine months later I bumped into him in the street, and did not recognize him. He called my name. I looked with disbelief at his

thin, crooked body, his grey hair and scarred face. 'I am Hassan
. . . Remember me?' he whispered. 'What have they done to you?' I
said. His eyes were as sad, as kind and as angry as ever. They have
managed to break his body, but not his soul. And I remember the
missing, the tortured and the killed in the Arab world . . .

Hana,[14] thin and petite, looked at me with her penetrating eyes.
She has always been thin, but the seven months she had spent
in Kuwait City since the invasion had made her even thinner.
She cleared her voice and said, 'Remember me? I lived most of
my life in Western cities, where I studied languages and other
cultures. Often we would discuss feminism and the rights of
women. Well, things have changed since. My whole life has
turned upside down since the 2nd of August. On that day, a
Thursday, I woke up to the sound of jet fighters and within
hours the whole area was littered with Iraqi soldiers, tanks and
missiles. We were forced out of our house as the coast was
vacated for military use. As we left, I looked at the receding
skyline, and decided to stay in Kuwait. It is my country, where I
belong, and where I should stay.

'The first month was dreadful, we were terrified. We all lost
weight. We had to stay indoors and they came and searched our
houses. Dead bodies were put in the ice-skating rink.
Hundreds were arrested and interrogated in the stadium. It was
terrible. I started having nightmares and waking up in the
middle of the night, too scared to sleep again. We've got used
to hearing stories about friends dying and checkpoints . . .
endless checkpoints . . .

'Slowly, we got used to living under occupation. People
started looking for food. We are growing vegetables in the
garden now – cucumbers, tomatoes, onions, parsley and corn
. . . it keeps me sane while all around is violence and
destruction. I spend a lot of time with my nieces and nephews
and have learnt how to cook for myself and the family. After
years of Western-style feminism, I ended up cooking,

babysitting and sweeping the floors. I haven't changed, but my life has. I look around me and fail to recognize my home town. Everything is either looted or destroyed. Paintings of our new "leader" are everywhere. My country has changed . . . I cannot tell you more . . .'

## Jordan

And you watch your country, which used to be healthy and prosperous, turn into a poor beggar after the war. You watch Jordanian women struggling to feed their children, to keep their children in school. And you see Reem and Rabab, eight-year-old girls, exchanging uniforms quickly in the courtyard. They split up into morning and afternoon shifts because they have to share the same school uniform. Tomatoes have become the only fruit which Jordanians don't need to draw for their children. To pacify a son asking for an apple, a mother drew it for him and told him to imagine what it tastes like. You say it is the Africanization of your country. You ask me, 'Can you see the eyes of the hungry children? How can you describe the pain . . . ?'[15]

'I am a teacher from Jabal El-Nuzha, Amman.[16] The other day, Samir, an eight-year-old pupil of mine, looked sleepy in class. So I asked him to go to the blackboard and write something for me. He pulled himself out of the desk, and while walking to the board fell on the floor. We took him to the doctor. When he was alone with the doctor, he burst into tears and said, "I am starving. Please, please don't tell my mother." The doctor said there was nothing wrong with Samir, he was just hungry. I shared my breakfast with him; he was eating, crying, and saying, "My mother will kill me. She told me not to ask for food or accept food from anyone. 'Don't tell the neighbours we have nothing to eat,' she said."'

'Don't tell the neighbours I'm still waiting,' said Suha,[17] a young Jordanian girl. Her rounded face and gentle voice revealed her Syrian origins. 'It all started when I went to university. The year I spent in the Jordan valley studying agriculture was the best time of my life. Things have changed since then. In the Jordan valley, on the banks of a shallow water reservoir, I met Emad, a handsome, generous, soft-spoken Iraqi man who joined Jordan University during the Iran–Iraq War. While weeding, milking the cows and ploughing, I would steal a glance at his face. We were always together.

'After graduation, he was summoned by his government to join the army. Since then, I've only had snatches of news. "I am safe, on the front line. We are fighting for our country." Days pass and I still wait for Emad. All my friends have got married except me. After the end of the Iran–Iraq War, he sent me a note saying, "In nine months' time, I will be released from the army. I will come to Jordan and propose to your family, as soon as possible." After two months Saddam Hussein invaded Kuwait. I've heard nothing from him since. I believe he was sent to Kuwait along with other conscripts. I don't know whether he is still alive. But I saw the pictures on television – the faces of charred bodies on the road to Basra. I have not seen Emad's face for seven years now. I kept seeing the images of the road – the grins of scorched corpses, the cries of pain, the grief of Iraqi mothers. I remember Emad's brown eyes teasing me, loving me, and pray to God that they have not been burnt . . .'

## Iraq

And you[18] watch, without blinking, your home town, Baghdad, the capital of Haroun al-Rasheed, in the 'blitz'. And no one mentions the soldiers in the burnt-out tanks or the families in the rubble. And you say, 'I cannot go on, but I must go on.' You watch the family, the marketplace, the neighbourhood school and the palm tree, where you used to play with your childhood friends, being blown to pieces.

And when the first B-52 hits Baghdad, you take a deep breath.

You ask your friends to hold you. And we do. You can't stand watching the 'fireworks' any more. You start rummaging through your old sketchbooks to see if you have one of your old neighbourhood. You look everywhere and find nothing. 'I would have painted everything if I had known what would happen – the women, the children, the mosques, the schools, the houses, the bridges, the roads, the trees, the sky. If only I had known.' You say you have nothing left of Iraq apart from the landscape in the heart . . . and I look at your usually peaceful eyes and see them smouldering with anger.[19] You rub your hands together, your fingers like the wings of a captive bird. I kneel and thank whoever is up there that you did not go blind . . .

Umm-Rashid[20] stood in the middle of Basra, tall, silent, wrinkled and blind. Her black veil slipped back, revealing grey temples. 'I must whisper my story to you,' she said, 'the place is bugged . . . I cannot even talk to myself. My husband, Abu-Rashid, was killed in the Iran–Iraq War.[21] My eldest son Adel was called up and taken to the front. They told me two years later that he was "lost in action". I don't know what that's suppose to mean. Adel, like his father before him, has gone away, never to come back. His wife went back to her family in Safwan. She took the two boys with her.

'My second son Samir refused to join the army. In the middle of the night, the secret police came looking for him. One of them held Radi, his three-year-old son, and started pulling his ear. When one of them yanked his hair, Radi burst into tears. Samir kissed his wife's forehead, and then kissed my hand and went with them. I watched his bowing head until he disappeared into the darkness and I wondered if I would ever see him again. Radi stood shaking in the corner. Samir's wife could no longer feed her baby daughter – her milk had dried up. Concerned about my old age, she decided to stay with me. I went to the police station in Basra to look for Samir and they

told me that he had been sent to Kuwait, our nineteenth
province.

'Then the war started. American and English planes began
dropping bombs on us from the sky.[22] The bombardment
continued for weeks, my daughter, until we couldn't take it any
more. First the water went, so we had no water to drink or
flush the toilets. Then the electricity and telephones.
Enveloped in darkness, we sat in our house, the four of us,
listening to the bombers overhead. Where is Samir? Will
anyone tell me whether he is still alive? Is he in Kuwait? Can no
one tell me anything? His wife went silent. Her baby daughter
sucked at her empty bottle. The sound of her sucking, and the
rhythmic bombardment, echoed in my head. Enveloped in
candlelight, we spent our evenings waiting for the
bombardment and the noise to stop. Until one night our house
was hit. I was playing in the kitchen with Radi, who since the
beginning of the war had been afraid of being left alone. When
bits of ceiling started falling on our heads, we took to the floor.
I thought I heard a suppressed cry. Later, when I came round I
looked at the rubble. Everything was destroyed except the
kitchen. Radi started crying. With my bare hands I looked for
my daughter-in-law and her baby amongst the rubble. I found
nothing – not even a shred of cloth.

'Before long we got used to sleeping under the half-
destroyed roof of the kitchen. The nights were cold and Radi
hugged me as he slept on my lap. There was no water, no food,
no milk – no people. He started crying for food and water.
Risking my life, I ran down the alleyways looking for water. I
found a dirty puddle. I scooped some into a bucket and took it
back to the pile of rubble which used to be our house. The
water was dirty, but my grandchild was thirsty. 'Drink,' I said.
He drank. The next day he developed a fever and diarrhoea.
He was losing weight. I hugged him to keep him warm. There
were no people or doctors around. And this hell was still
pouring from the sky. It was a clear night when Radi whispered

through his dry lips, 'Grandma,' and died in my lap. I looked at the sky and saw nothing. No flashes of bombs and bullets, no rubble. Sitting on a stone, in what used to be our sitting-room, Praise be to Allah, I have gone blind . . .'[23]

I looked into my mother's eyes, which had witnessed the 1948 catastrophe, the 1967 Arab–Israeli War, the 1970 civil war and the Gulf War; her eyes which saw the pursuit of her husband and children by the secret police and are still smiling. 'It's time you learnt how to make a gas mask,' she said to me one evening as she laid the table for supper. She scooped some *labaneh* yoghurt from the dripping linen bag, laid the bread and salad on the table, and started giving me the recipe: 'First you soak the cloth in bleach, then stuff it with sponge and carbon.' She continued as if describing a delicious Middle Eastern dish: 'The first one you make might not be sealed, but you'll learn.'

## Notes

1. In her book *War's Other Voices: Women Writers on Lebanese Civil War 1977–82* (Cambridge University Press, 1988) Miriam Cooke argues that most Arab women, like women everywhere, perceive war differently from Arab men. Whereas men, positioned at the conflict's epicentre, perceive war in 'terms of strategy, ideology and violence', the women, from their situation at the margins, experience the 'dailiness of war'.

2. *Al-Raai*, 28 March 1991.

3. Most Arab women in the twentieth century have not only suffered external conflict – the four Arab–Israeli wars and the struggle for independence – but also, with the emergence of the nation-state in the Arab world, the internal hardship of totalitarian rule. For more details see 'Women and Politics', *Middle East Report*, no. 138, January–February 1986.

4. According to the *Jerusalem Star*, Vol. 2, no. 33, 8 March 1984, Jordanian women were given the right to elect and be elected in March 1973. They exercised that right for the first time in the 1984 by-elections. Kuwaiti women still do not have the right to elect and be elected.

5. On 15 June 1982, Ein el-Helweh camp was destroyed by Israeli

forces, causing thousands of civilian casualties. For more details see Dina Abdel Hamid's *Duet for Freedom*, London: Quartet, 1988.

6. On 9 June 1982, Beirut was subjected by the Israeli air force to one of the biggest air battles over its skies. Three days of bombardment left 7,000 dead and wounded.

7. Umm-Khalid, 'the mother of Khalid', the usual Arab naming pattern, Khalid being her eldest son.

8. About a third of the two million Palestinian population in Israel are in prison.

9. Between 16 January and 17 March 1991, the Israeli government banned the 60,000 Palestinian workers from crossing the Green Line between the occupied territories and Israel. Most of these Palestinians work in construction, agriculture and restaurants (*al-Quds*, 18 March 1991).

10. 400,000 Palestinians used to work in Kuwait before the Iraqi invasion, mainly in education, health and construction.

11. 6,000 Palestinians, out of the 170,000 who decided to stay in Kuwait after the Iraqi invasion, were arrested after the liberation of Kuwait. According to *al-Quds*, 8 March 1991, many of the Palestinians captured were tortured, subjected to summary justice and executed. These reports were confirmed by Amnesty International, the Red Cross and other reports. See Simon Tisdall's 'Kuwaiti reign of terror against Palestinians', the *Guardian*, 22 March 1991.

12. Umm-Ramadan's account and part of the section on Kuwait are based on Amnesty International's *Iraq/Occupied Kuwait: Human Rights Violations since 2 August* (19 December 1990).

13. See Amnesty International, *Iraq – Children: Innocent Victims of Political Repression* (February 1989) and Middle East Watch, *Human Rights in Iraq* (February 1990).

14. This account is loosely based on information smuggled out of Kuwait in December 1990 from Kuwaiti women friends who decided to stay in Kuwait and brave the occupation of their country.

15. Jordan has lost 77 per cent of its Gross Domestic Product during the war, 30 per cent of its 3.1 million population are under the poverty line and 40 per cent, mainly women, are unemployed. For more details about the plight of Jordan see UNICEF, *Jordanian Children in the Eye of the Storm* (February 1991).

16. *Al-Raai*, 11 March 1991.

17. A faithful description of the plight of a Jordanian friend. I have changed the names to protect the persons involved.

18. This is based on many first-hand accounts of expatriate and exiled Iraqi women. There are about 10,000 Iraqis living in Britain, many of whom are either writers or artists.

19. See Alfonso Rojo's 'Angry eyes of a woman, sad eyes of a child, all accusing', the *Guardian*, 2 February 1991.

20. Umm-Rashid's plight is based on *WHO/UNICEF Special Mission to Iraq* (February 1991) and the coverage of the Gulf War by both the *Independent* and the *Guardian*, especially articles by Nora Boustany of the *Washington Post*, Robert Fisk and Alfonso Rojo of the Spanish *El Mundo*.

21. There are conflicting accounts about the number of Iraqi soldiers who died in the Iran–Iraq War. Some estimates puts it as high as 200,000.

22. In the forty-two days of fighting, the amount of explosives the Allies dropped on Iraq was roughtly equivalent to four times the amount dropped on Hiroshima.

23. Some Vietnamese women suffered a psychologically induced blindness as a result of what they had witnessed during the Vietnam War.

# HAIFAA KHALAFALLAH

## *Egypt's Central Role*

Saddam Hussein's blunder with the invasion of Kuwait thrust Egypt into the centre of the Middle East stage. Egypt provided the mandate for the Western–Arab alliance against Iraq and the use of Western forces against that country.

Had Saudi Arabia and Syria joined the chorus of the peripheral states which opposed the war, without Egypt supporting the war, the Western alliance would still have had the legitimacy, if not all the military access it needed. Similarly, had Egypt sided with Iraq, or even remained neutral, the legality of the US-led coalition would have been questionable, if not impossible. It also legitimized the 'Arab alliance' and gave it the weight that the other 'Arab-alliance' against the war could not match.

In the Gulf crisis of August 1990, with its suddenness and confused issues, Egypt's choice (right or wrong) decided who were the good guys and who were the bad guys. Without it, the use of Western forces in the region would have been either unthinkable or a prelude to an all-out war. In 1990, all the Arab partners to the Gulf conflict, including Iraq, worked within a framework defined by Egyptian choices. The Iraqi attendance of the Arab league meetings in Cairo is a testimony to that.

Lord Cromer, the nineteenth-century British Consul-General and effective ruler of Egypt, could not have foreseen this Egyptian role. He insisted that Egypt did not constitute a genuine nation and therefore could not aspire to an independent national existence.[1] In his second volume on *Modern Egypt*, Lord Cromer described the 'tortuous' nature of the 'oriental' mind, especially its 'inveterate' love of intrigue. He contrasted this nature with that of the British: 'who, perhaps more than any other, loathe and despise intrigue; who, in their dealings with their fellow-men, are frank and blunt.'[2] Cromer's wisdom notwithstanding, Egyptian nationalism has proved to be not only a formidable force in the region, but perhaps the most viable of all Middle East national allegiances today. As for the alleged 'tortuous' nature, history is a better judge.

Egypt's weight had become evident in recent years well before the Gulf crisis. When the Rejectionist Front, led by Baghdad in 1979, organized an Egyptian boycott in protest at the Camp David Agreement and Egypt's peace with Israel, the political map of the region was hardly affected by that loud chest-beating: The Camp David Agreement is still in force, while the Rejectionist Front has disbanded. And when Iranian victories threatened all the Arab Gulf states, both internally and externally, the same Rejectionist Front, led by Baghdad, turned to Cairo: Saddam Hussein, 'the defender of the Arabs', proved unable to defend himself. It was Egypt's support and propaganda machine that tipped the scale in favour of Iraq during that earlier military blunder of Saddam Hussein.

Because of the Gulf crisis, now however, Egypt finds itself in the midst of difficult and threatening dilemmas. The resolution – or lack of resolution – of these dilemmas will have far-reaching effects not only on the Gulf but on any 'new' or even old Middle East order.

The first dilemma is moral – it is also an Arab dilemma. Defects have arisen in the conscience of the once-powerful idea of Arab nationalism and contemporary Arab intellect. Theories of regional systems and balance of power may be useful for academicians in distant places to explain Arab myopia. Nevertheless, the lack of protest over the ten-year war against Iran, the 1988 gassing of the

Kurds, the flagrant violation of civil rights, the low value of human life – especially Arab life – raise difficult questions that need answers.

Egypt's role is paramount in all this moral crisis. It supported Saddam Hussein during one wasteful and cruel war and then only watched as he held back the savings of Egypt's blue-collar workers in Iraq and even executed several Egyptians as they attempted to send their income home. Egyptians are unlikely to forget this.

Egypt later formed the focus for opposition against this same Saddam Hussein in his other cruel and wasteful war. In doing so, however, it took a step unprecedented in its long history. Egyptians have had a historical responsibility towards the region. Others could afford to take sides recklessly, but not Egypt. To take up arms with French, British and American soldiers (to be in the same warring camp with Israel) against destitute and oppressed Iraqi men and women is a negation of its history. This action will, for a long time, trouble Egyptian consciences as the defeat in Palestine did in the beginning of the second half of this century.

Egyptian and other Arab intellectuals are now asking themselves inevitable questions about the future: Where did we go wrong, intellectually and morally? Is this the end of 'Arab' history? What does 'Arab' mean in the light of the new developments? Is it a reference to culinary and musical traditions, or is it a reference to an existing community – even if not yet translated in political terms – that shares one language, a long heritage, rich religious experiences and common political aspirations?

If there is no such community, then where does Egypt stand, at least culturally? That cultural choice is no secondary issue: it could determine the predominant and new culture of the region.

The second dilemma is economic. Hundreds of thousands of Egyptian workers are back home from the Gulf. That 'middle class' of economically prosperous Egyptians (they include both white- and blue-collar workers) are now without jobs, without their life savings, without their comfortable modern apartments, without schools for their children. They have no immediate prospects of relief. Kuwait, for one, is unable and perhaps unwilling to take them back. Iraq also offers little short-term hope. Unemployed and frustrated by its sudden and severe change of fortunes, this group, which was until recently one of the country's major sources of foreign currency and wealth, spells economic and social problems for Egypt.

The crisis of that large group of Egyptians is not being seriously addressed. Who is responsible for their immediate help and long-term well-being? The Egyptian government profited from their wealth but does not have much of its own now to alleviate their condition. The Gulf governments, including Iraq and Kuwait, benefitted from their long years of hard work but at the moment have their own economic woes and priorities. The answer is far from clear.

What is clear is that they are accorded low priority on the agenda of Egyptian and Gulf governments. This could prove to be a costly mistake, because they, as well as their fellow-countrymen with whom they now compete for nonexistent jobs, living space, schools, or just a place on public transport, are the most likely group to effect profound changes for all those governments.

The third dilemma is political. Since the 1952 revolution Egypt has had to adjust its internal and external political visions more than once. However, the general framework in which those varying visions were grounded remained the same. This framework included a consensus that monarchy is an unjust institution of government; that 'democracy' and social justice are the ultimate goals of the Egyptian revolutionary spirit; and that in spite of all setbacks, that revolutionary spirit has won most of its major battles – especially its long struggle for independence from foreign powers. Finally, Egypt represents Egyptian interests and policies only.

The Free Officers, Najeeb, Nasser, Sadat and Mubarek, may have had different recipes for how to run their society but the thrust and legitimacy of that evolving Egyptian 'revolution' has never been renounced by any of them, least of all Sadat. But with the new political order that resulted from the 1990 Gulf crisis,

Egypt suddenly looks more like its pre-1952 self: an anchor for the status quo in the region. Is the Egyptian revolutionary thrust over? How does Egypt stand *vis-à-vis* the region and the world? Is it officially aiming at the preservation of the feudal systems of government in the region, which it had previously, at least implicitly, viewed as unacceptable? Is Egypt officially a Western ally? And if so, how does this affect the Egyptian – or Arab – social and political aspirations?

With sixty centuries of history, the Egyptians cannot help but have a long memory. The political lessons of modern times include one learnt from another Hussein – Sharif Hussein, the so-called Sheriff of Mecca. The story of his alliance with Britain during World War I and his Arab revolt against Ottoman rule is sobering: it is a reminder of what the outcome of an alliance with Western powers is likely to accomplish for the interest of the region or its politicians.[3]

The Arab army of 1916–18 (more effective than those of 1991) came to the valuable aid of the British, who 'woke up to the fact that the Arabs could be knit together into a fighting force of real value and relied upon to pin down the Turks East of the Jordan River . . .'[4]

After the Allied victory the Turkish nightmare was replaced by the spectre of Western colonial rule which resulted, among other things, in the 'topsy-turvy division of Syria and Iraq . . .' and other parts of the region.

Ironically, it seems that those who kept some distance from Western fights were those who benefited most; Ibn Saud, as compared with Sharif Hussein, presents a clear case in point.

Another lesson was delivered in the Iran–Iraq War: a proxy war waged by Saddam Hussein, paid for by Saudi Arabia, Kuwait and the United Arab Emirates, on behalf of the US, which had been humiliated by Khomeini and was attempting to bring the strategically important Iran back into a co-operative mood. With its history still unwritten, the outcome of that war is quickly unravelling: the Kuwaiti Foreign Minister is said to have apologized to the Iranians in August 1990 and on 16 August Saddam Hussein gave back all Iraq's territorial gains and agreed to return to the 1975 Algeria treaty.

Sad ironies abound: from the Iran–Contra affair, to the story of the Kuwaiti newspaper which fervently proclaimed Hussein 'the defender of Arabs against Persian threats' during the 1980s and then watched his army, on 8 August 1990, select its building for occupation by his troops and move on to loot its expensive modern printing presses.

One must wonder: what if the Arab political system, or even the Arab intellectual establishment, had tried to work out a *modus vivendi* with the Iranian revolution – to assure the prosperity of both peoples – based on regional interests and not on those of the USA? After all, the Arab world shares much common ground with its difficult neighbour. Perhaps the exorbitant human and economic price paid by the citizenry of Kuwait, Iraq, Iran and other countries of the Middle East would have been avoided. One thing is certain, however: for its people, nothing could have been worse than the eventual outcome. There is no man, woman or child in the region who has escaped the events of the past ten years without some serious harm.

To avoid a repeat of the blunders of the Hussein of World War I, those of the Hussein of the Iran–Iraq 1980s war and the Kuwait 1990–91 war, to avoid new entanglements in the Western web of intrigues and conspiracies and threats to the region's wealth, Arabs, privately, know that their only hope resides now in Egypt. Egypt can 'peacefully' keep at bay any threats to the sovereignty of the Arab region. It has the demographic and cultural depths as well as the political weight.

But this can happen only if Egypt is strong and prosperous. Also, the Egyptian leadership must remain aware of two factors: its role as the last fort in resistance against the new sweeping pressures of foreign entanglements and the need, at the same time, to keep 'friendly' relations with the leading powers of that 'new world order', or whatever world order is likely to emerge from the turbulent 1990s.

To think of itself as just another country in the region, like Qatar or Bahrain, or even Saudi Arabia or Syria, is to stall peace efforts and endanger Arab interests. Furthermore, in insisting on preserving the status quo in the region, Egypt is avoiding its responsibilities. Like everyone else, Egypt knows that social and political changes are long overdue in the Middle East. Minimal civil and human rights are not marginal 'bourgeois niceties', but urgent priorities that should head the agenda of necessary reforms.

That need for change is unquestionable. A senior and conservative official from an Arab royal family privately noted in December 1990, during a dinner given in his honour in London, that 'this Gulf crisis proved without a shadow of doubt that the old order is out'. A bold journalist asked if that included his royal family. 'Among others, but the tragedy will be trying to hold on against an overwhelming tide of change,' he predicted.

Unlike the USA, which sits thousands of miles from the region and possesses a minuscule historical perspective, those who actually live in the Middle East understand the danger and complexity of the tensions in the region – tensions that are aggravated by two decades of 'cash prosperity' but also by political, economic and civil deprivation. These tensions have undermined any sense of security and resulted in an identity crisis. The irony is that these identity and security crises are so acute in the Arab region but at the same time so irrelevant to the rest of the world. This paradox makes unthinkable chaos a likely outcome in the Middle East – so long as peacful change towards economic as well as political justice is not given a chance.

## Notes

1. Albert Hourani, *Arabic Thought in the Liberal Age: 1798–1939*, Oxford: Oxford University Press, 1970, p. 198.

2. Lord Cromer, *Modern Egypt*, vol II, p. 151.

3.  Sharif Hussein engaged in a correspondence with Sir Henry McMahon, then British Agent in Cairo, since 1915, in which the British government promised their support for the Arabs in their attempts to gain their freedom and independence from the Ottoman rulers. At the same time Britain had signed a secret agreement with France, the Sykes-Picot Agreement, in which the two countries divided greater Syria and Iraq among themselves. Also, at the same time, A. J. Balfour, the British Foreign Secretary, issued a pledge to European Jewry, in 1917, in which he promised them a 'national home' in Palestine once the war was over – in an attempt to subvert French influence in the region.

4.  Anthony Nutting, *The Arabs*, New York: Clarkson N. Potter, 1964, p. 288.

# EDWARD PEARCE

## *War-Guilt, Zinoviev and the Boring Canadian: The Press and The War*

History to the defeated must say 'alas'

The hard dismissal which W. H. Auden, in his shallow Marxist phase, first offered and then recanted, fits the attitude to the Gulf War of press and government, in Britain at least. The defeated, of course, are the dead: Iraqi conscript soldiers, peasants in uniform, the baked smiling mud face in the tank turret. The other quote which Auden lived to disown referred to 'the necessary murder.'

All war is a failure of imagination. Few wars can have been more marked than this by unwillingness to make the imaginative jump from military display and preparation to the burnt-out dead-littered aftermath. The press and television have been broadly good at illustrating apolitical peacetime human suffering – though I recall the indignation and outrage in the *Daily Telegraph* leader editorial conference at the evil-doing of Michael Buerk when his team of cameramen on their way back from South Africa stopped off in Ethiopia and delineated the suffering of starving people there. This depiction was considered by *Telegraph* leader-writers to constitute many things: emotional self-indulgence, intrusion into private comfort, deep-seated left-wing conspiracy of an undefined sort and simple ungentlemanly conduct. Similar objections were made to the baked face in the tank turret.

Pictures are almost everything in argument. They fly where the most formidable words can only plod. They are *momenti mori*, reminders of death. And in talking about starvation or war, we do not remember death. Only shock of the crudest kind makes us mindful of it. Accordingly, the debate leading up to the war was strangely thin. It chiefly concerned *our* safety. Would we win safely enough, would our boys be not much endangered? Would there be elements of the Vietnam experience – meaning would war go on for an interminable time, creating weariness as we enmired ourselves there? As anyone might have pointed out at once, there was no such prospect.

Iraq is not a power except in terms of her neighbours and her still less lucky citizens. This was always going to be a fight between the United States and her followers against a medium-sized Middle Eastern despotism with delusions. The official government view, faithfully echoed in the press, was to take Iraq at her own absurd valuation. For the purposes of legitimizing what was always going to be a shooting-gallery war, it was apt and convenient to let Saddam Hussein's balcony rhetoric pass as sober analysis of strength, and paper estimates of weaponry and troop strengths assume maximum proportions. That the weapons were safely sold and last year's models, and the troops either glorified secret policemen or coerced conscripts, was never spelt out. Men certain of a triumph are inclined to promote the dimensions of the dragon encountered.

The phrase about a 'turkey shoot', coined by the dreadful old man of the *Sunday Times*, Norman Macrae, and adopted in fugal form at the war's end by their resident sensibility-grinder Norman Stone, was more than a brutish exaltation of the joys of killing; it gave the game away comprehensively. To what end is war being presented as a mighty encounter and soldiers serenaded as gallant lads running fearful dangers, if ordinarily non-specialist advocates of the same war can recognize it for a killer's doddle? There may not be much sensitivity about the possible wrongs of war in Britain, but one can hardly say 'Let us go and fight an easy war with negligible risks and simple targets'. What are *Te Deums* for, to what end do we hold ceremonial march pasts or call on the Queen to thank God in our deliverance?

One cannot decently proclaim a coming bout with an accredited underdog. Despite Orwell's gloomy view that older notions of chivalry were being transformed by realpolitik and that Jack the Giantkiller would be replaced by Jack the Dwarfkiller, no one can go so far (though there was the 'journalist' who confided to a camera crew before broadcasting that he 'couldn't wait for us to start bombing wogs').

Broadly, we understated Western strength. Endless hours were given over to discussions about Iraqi potential and how to cope with it. Given such an approach, appropriate for the run-up to a match between the champion and what Joe Louis used to call his 'bum of the month', a false notion of war was created from which would derive a false notion of victory. Because we would not concede our superiority, there was nothing in debate of Samuel Johnson's contempt, more than two hundred years ago, for 'the wickedness of making war on savage peoples' ('savage' meaning for him roughly what 'Third World' means for us).

Possibly this may explain the difference between reactions to the Gulf and those thirty-five years earlier to the Suez invasion. The Labour Party, patriotically primed for war, trying in every way to look 'fit to govern' in the patronizing term of the Conservatives and living up to the tone set by Neil Kinnock's imitation regimental tie, was in enlightening contradistinction to Hugh Gaitskell in Trafalgar Square making public protest against war. (The thought also occurs that moral authority comes from self-confidence, which Gaitskell's party, not long out of office, still had, while Kinnock's thrice-beaten commanders of 31 per cent last time do not.)

But in 1956 the war looked like great-power arrogance against a menial state. In 1991 the Western puffing of Iraq's status, 'the fourth-strongest power in the world', gave to a colonial expedition a useful moral gloss. There is something else – the poor world, the Third World, the remote victims of poverty and war, constitute excellent moral wallpaper or table music for our more enlightened moments. But to all but the very engaged or very sensitive they are remote in the way of other constellations. The point of a picture is.

99

that it condenses death into a shocking icon, teaches the wrongness of such undertakings. Two pictures shone out of the Vietnam War – one showed a child, burnt with napalm, running screaming down a road; the other an officer holding a revolver to the temple of a man whose arms were tied behind his back. Useless to argue that the victim was a terrorist or that the Tet Offensive during which this killing occurred was marked with even worse Viet Cong atrocities. The pictures simply said 'War is like this'. They were met with a great antiphon: 'We want no more of it'. The unpolitical American public did not learn any specific points about that war or general principles about war as such; they learnt immediate revulsion.

The whole point about the makers of war in the Gulf was that they understood perfectly that irrational disgust at the necessary business of killing people in order to win would in due course operate against them. Accordingly, the only good war, the only just war, the only war right for electoral purposes, is a short one. Even if the death toll is very heavy, it will work providing there is expedition and dispatch. A hundred thousand Iraqi soldiers killed in weeks, either under a bombardment which included Fuel Air Explosives or by deliberate strafing of men in comprehensive retreat, makes up a vast question. We responded by not even contemplating it.

'But we always knew that war was hell,' said the lady from the *Daily Mail* with a toss of her head. 'They invaded Kuwait,' said the Conservative lady Euro MP. The ability for spokespeople to fall into perfect autism in the face of our side's wrongdoing is profoundly impressive. The people who had been against the war were shocked by the killing, but then we would be, wouldn't we? Ironically, in the week when the war demonstrated specifically and categorically that all argument for it had been invalid – easy victory over hopeless adversary, gratuitous slaughter, use by America of chemical weapons, mighty destruction of the environment, an armful of dust and bone shard at the end of our endeavours – fools stepped forward to proclaim that the war's opponents had been proved wrong and what did they have to say to that? It is an argument which could have been used with propriety in Chicago on the morning after St Valentine's Day.

In fairness, the sort of mind operating in the Oval Office and the Pentagon had more in common with the crasser kind of American rules football coach. *Vae victis* is a useful guide to custom and practice in world affairs, but it is not a moral precept.

What shone out of the great killings of January and February 1991 was the absence of any very active sense of wrong in America and to a still greater extent in Britain. A hundred thousand dead make a great thing. Men might ponder those dead and set them against whatever had been gained – the influence of the USA among her Arab allies, the reassurance of Saudi Arabia, the gains for the Republican Party – and they might weigh them against the hundred thousand and make a judgement.

But the dead have had no impact and must find other dead to bury them. One might make play in the manner of the reflexive left and see a racial aspect to this response. Could we have so lightly borne (or so lightly killed) a hundred thousand Swedes or Czechs or even rather off-white Spaniards? In the bills of mortality there are unacknowledged weightings of which lives matter rather more. But I would prefer the lesser prejudice of distance; a remote victim, even vastly multiplied, is less pain to us. It used to be said that a million dead in Chinese floods were less immediate and thus less pitiful than a single child drowned in a pond. And indeed, a single Chinese or Iraqi child burnt dead in a house fire here in England would engage more of our sympathy than the hundred thousand killed, many of them scorched or asphixiated by Fuel Air Explosives, the chemical weapons used by the USA's dinky little portable Dresdens whose fireball effect suffocates what they don't burn up. Distance is one part of our indifference, lack of imagination another part. We have the means to kill, but perhaps not the means to mind.

For conducting such a war the British press is perfectly equipped. It can, at its Cro-Magnon level – all shambling gait, protruding lower jaw and hair on the back of its hands – denounce the bastards who hold our boys; it can call for us to 'nuke Baghdad'. The British lower press is a sort of parody prole in type whose creators seem to model themselves on the press in *Nineteen Eighty-Four* saluting the latest victories in the wars which Oceania must fight – now with Eurasia against hateful Eastasia, now with Eastasia against abominable Eurasia. Look at the last ten years in the Middle East – at Iran and Iraq, Iraq and Iran, and – handy dandy – which is which?

Paul Johnson, with his 'Prayer for our boys' in the *Daily Mail*, is a figure clean out of dystopic fiction, the converted leftist doing a lifelong public penance by performances which would not have disgraced the accused at a Moscow show trial proclaiming his love of Stalin. The *Daily Mail*, having first published the Zinoviev letter,[1] now goes one better and has Zinoviev on retainer.

But our supposed quality press is no better. One expects nothing from the *Times*, always a humble and amenable servant of power, its tired cache of columnists and its heavy-laden leader-writers all standing by their beds in the fashion of private soldiers. From the *Times* one expects bright-eyed mediocrity, and gets it. But all the serious papers – the *Guardian* excepted – were for war, the Sundays being for it in the way that a football supporter of the Stanley-knife-carrying sort is for next Saturday's away match. What one notices there is an intense admiration for the United States as such, pride in American strength, an exaltation of war and a collapse of all good manners. The description in the *Sunday Times* after the war of Bobby Muller – the Vietnam veteran who campaigns against the war from the wheelchair to which his spinal cord severed on active service has confined him – as 'a cardboard cut-out cripple' is morally at one with the same paper's degraded 'turkey shoot' and suggests that hypocrisy is a much-underrated virtue.

For the *Independent*, intense bobbysoxing admiration of all things American on the part of a couple of its personages explains much, but the contrast between the news coverage from the likes of

Robert Fisk, chronicler of the long kill in Lebanon, and the relaxed, soft-shoe bellicism of a London office content to take its prejudices on stage, was notable.

With a press so ready for war, with war itself physically remote and with the waging of it one of the few areas in which The British still excel, our uncritical happiness with the killing ought not to surprise anyone. But as the aftermath of war takes its ironic turns, one watches our press for signs. Signs of repentance, perhaps? Well, the boring Canadian in the *Observer* who droned on about the propriety of war before it started is honourably upset at the Kurds being massacred and George Bush standing by like patience on a monument, showing how bravely he can take it.

The editorialists of the *Independent* and the *Sunday Times*, having been breathless for war, certainly want Saddam Hussein stopped from the killing which a war against his evil has left him doing rather more of. So they might, so they might. For press and government alike, the survival of Saddam Hussein to become again the preferred option of Foreign Offices ('Strong man better than internal anarchy, old boy') is a sort of exercise in just how low a temperature cold blood may run at.

It is hard to resist an observation that for the British broadly, war has come to play a therapeutic role. We have not enjoyed the successes of the Germans, the Italians or the French in commercial terms. The Workshop of the World, whose eighteenth- and nineteenth-century industrial leaders were often fascinatingly pacific, has been undersold and outproduced. Morale is low and commercially we are a laggard, incapable of putting together the production, sales and maintenance standards which create a strong currency and a virtuous circle of economic strength. Yet ironically, the armed forces (together, oddly, with agriculture) are very good, lean, proficient, technically very literate, able to select highly motivated, very capable soldiers. If our cars were like our combat regiments, the Japanese would be sitting up.

It is human nature to play to strengths, less excusable to seek solace in the destructive talents we command. But the British outlook could almost be summed up as 'We don't have a BMW, so let's rely on the SAS'. The Falklands first and now the Gulf War have given us a fillip, made us seem more important than we are. In better times it was the misfit, the individual failure, who 'went for a soldier'. The singularly bitter truth is that a country has gone for a soldier, or at least has done so from time to time. Remote wars unrelated to true security can conjure up a happy condition – a high, almost a false notion of being beleaguered and threatened, with the comforting knowledge that we are nothing of the sort. Little wars are a snug and cosy palliative for our condition, a watered-down laudanum through whose haze we imagine and dream what is not. Foreign policy as fix is not to be recommended.

The advocates of war invoked Saddam Hussein's murderous record, which they had blithely ignored for a decade. They invoked it much as they might send out for prawn vindaloo with plain boiled rice and a nan and onion bhaji. They didn't, in their offices, believe in the indignation thing. Comforted by the knowledge that they had interests, not friends, inclined – in the USA – to say of two dozen assorted heads of state, 'He's a bastard but he's our bastard', they allowed themselves, for reasons only of agitation and propaganda, to play the moral card. And as Saddam Hussein, after shelling hospitals, murdering prisoners and dropping sulphuric acid on the Kurds, survives, they are irked to find that card adhering to unwilling fingers.

Somehow they must get back to amoral insouciance – fast. It shouldn't prove too hard. The people who brought you Augusto Pinochet by way of direct intervention in a sovereign state had no problem being shocked at Saddam Hussein and making interference with a sovereign state a *casus belli*. Explaining to us that intervention inside Iraq would prejudice the sovereignty they cherish and that Saddam Hussein though a bad thing, represents a force for stability should be well within the scope of any good professional.

Those of us who opposed the war did so out of a supposition that no good would come of it. None did. We did not believe the high moral line being taken as justification by people scornful of abstract morality. We were dead right. We thought that great numbers of remote, little-regarded peasants would die, and they have died. Worse things happened in the final days of the war and in the period following revolt in Iraqi provinces than the bleakest minds of us war-haters had conceived of.

The Americans will see that their nation, with the instincts of a continental parish armed for the annihilation of the universe, has used its giant's strength in the customary fearful way Shakespeare had in mind. Trusting in generals to seize power for American ends in Iraq, it has seen Kurds and Shiites, with rotten selfishness, pursue power for Kurdish and Shiite ends. These people appear, as I write in late March 1991, to have inherited the mercy of Saddam Hussein, the attention span of the Western media and the trustworthiness of George Bush.

The position of the press in March is dodgy. They cannot plead reasons of state for hightailing their way out of the moral certainties of yesterday into the world-forgetting oblivion of today. They are obliged to report the horrors of Basra and Kirkuk, and they are caught in mid-gesture frozen into an On To Baghdad gesture for all the world like a more than usually foolish-looking equestrian statue. Doubtless, if President Bush sticks with his current cold-eyed posture – one peculiarly apt for Easter, if you think about it – the press will find its own way out. It may, at the liberal fringe – *Observer* and *Independent* – revert to a measure of critical autonomy. Such gestures can be afforded since, after all, they would actually be supporting another gesture.

Those of us against the war of first instance need not now call upon George Bush to finish it off. Saddam Hussein's bombing of Kirkuk could have been stopped without a shot being fired. Such is the superiority of men and *matériel* that US and British aircraft need only fly immune over that city to indicate to Saddam Hussein's planes – and, indeed, to his investing land troops – to go no further. The USA has suasion in Iraq; it can say 'Do this' or 'Do not do this'. There is no indication, as I write, that such suasion will be exercised for the Kurds otherwise facing the psychopathic revenge of Saddam Hussein. A war was fought for face and command, for the power-clutching Sabah family of Kuwait. The energies of a dozen newspaper editors flying in formation have been bent nightly to the proclamation that, not only was this right but that those – like the Germans – shying away from it were despicable extesticular wimps.

If Bush does nothing and the Kurds continue to die horribly, one will be dreadfully embarrassed for the editors, but don't grieve. Time heals all things. The Kurds will be dead and the newspapers will have forgotten. That is what foreign coverage means. Newspapers have learnt anyway, in the best Horatio Bottomley style, to make heroes and oracles out of military commanders. They will have had the warm satisfaction of hearing the sensible voice of that bluff soldier Sir Peter de la Billiere proclaim, 'This is something which does not concern us'.

The press, callers up of a war, running footmen of the new world order, ignorers of firestorms, men with the sensibilities of pit props, will understand the profound wisdom of that gallant old soldier and will endeavour to live up to it. The expedition, so vitally right and good in their columns, conjured up dead upon dead and war upon war; cholera and late, long-burning fires command centre stage and Saddam Hussein rules. But it would be a bit naff to admit to having been wrong, wouldn't it? The press who brought you fevered coverage will shortly bring you the perfect forgetfulness which best accommodates foreigners suffering and dying ostentatiously in what is anyway a very remote and uninteresting country. They are, after all, none of our business.

## Note

1. The publication in 1924 of a letter allegedly from the Soviet politician Grigori Zinoviev (later murdered by Stalin) purporting to instruct Western fellow-travellers, including the British Labour Party, was an early draft of McCarthy-style smearing.

# DR LESLEY MORRISON

## The NHS and its Patients: Casualties of the Gulf War

**A** doctor aims to give his or her patient as much honest information as he or she wants and needs, to encourage participation in the decision about future course of management and to offer support in that decision. Patients (and the public) have the right to know the facts, as they can best be understood at that time; they have the right to choose.

The people of this country had little real choice about whether they went to war. War was presented as the only reasonable option. The other therapeutic alternatives were not discussed. Trust is essential for any therapeutic or management relationship, and the trust of the British people and National Health Service employees in what the government says about the NHS has been irreversibly damaged.

From several months before the war started, there was evidence that preparations for the reception of casualties on a massive scale were being made, but these preparations were shrouded in official secrecy. On 3 December 1990, responding to parlimentary questions, Secretary of State for Health Virginia Bottomley stated that no guidance had yet been given to NHS burns and plastic surgery units, or to any other NHS medical service in relation to Gulf casualties, despite the fact that by then civilian patients normally treated in military hospitals were being discharged/reallocated wherever possible, forming an additional immediate burden on the NHS; that by then 1,000 units of blood per day, with a shelf life of thirty-five days, were being sent to British field hospitals in Saudi

Arabia; that the Ministry of Defence had written early in December to all medical personnel in the Territorial Army (peacetime reservists) asking them to volunteer urgently for active service. There was indeed a gulf between what the government knew and what it was telling us, the people who would have to treat the sick and injured.

Then, in early January 1991, a restricted contingency planning document, published by the Department of Health on 14 December but not actually dispatched to district health authorities for another two weeks (Operation Granby),[1] was leaked and the government's true expectations about the impending burden on the NHS were revealed.

'The total numbers of casualties likely to build up in particular regions could show some increase over previous estimates.' The purpose of the plan was to treat UK armed forces casualties in NHS hospitals when Ministry of Defence resources could no longer cope. There were believed to be some 5,000 UK military personnel in the Gulf. A system of triage would apply. Seriously injured servicepeople were expected to be held for up to four days after initial surgery in the Gulf and then flown to England, either through Cyprus or directly. P3 category casualties would be those able to withstand a delay of more than twelve hours in receiving treatment; for them, there would be a three-stage build-up – stage 1 (days 1–2) mainly to service hospitals; stage 2 (days 2–5) mostly to the NHS; stage 3 (day 6 onwards) continued NHS support if needed. Earlier NHS involvement was anticipated if the Ministry of Defence was 'unable to maintain UK service hospitals as a "buffer"' – that is, if the MOD hospitals filled up. It was estimated that the NHS would have a minimum warning time of around one day plus twelve to fifteen hours' flight time to vacate beds. A 're-entry' stage was envisaged during which the backlog of NHS work and attention to routine waiting lists could begin to be picked up.

A clear statement was made: 'Once casualties start to arrive, at least 65–70 vacant beds per region per day might be needed in each region – over, say, five days – (and about twice that number in one or two regions occasionally) until the total of around 500 admissions has been reached for the region.'

A very interesting paragraph appeared towards the end of the document in a section entitled 'The Media'. If the press approached hospitals with inquiries 'for speculative articles', the 'line to take' was specified: 'Health authority contingency plans already provide for NHS casualties in the event of hostilities. Regional General Managers have been asked to consider what preparatory measures might be needed under the plans.' In other words, the line to take was to withhold information about specific plans which had been made. A covering letter which was distributed with the document by one regional health authority stated: 'In particular, no impression should be given to the press or public that NHS beds are being cleared for military casualties . . .'

What, in truth, was happening? Ashford Hospital near Staines, as one example, planned to 'discharge as many of our existing in-patients as possible' and 'cancel all except urgent and emergency admissions' in the event of war.

On 28 December 1990 the Department of Health published another circular to 'Senior Staff in Confidence', 'Gulf Contingency Planning: NHS Medical Guide'. It described the type and extent of injuries anticipated and methods of treatment. It admitted for the first time that 'There is likely to be heavy pressure on burns, intensive care and neurosurgery units' which 'may arise, in part, from staff shortages, particularly of nurses and technicians. Nurses in burns units need special skills and training and cannot be recruited *ad hoc*.' It also prepared hospitals for a wide range of chemical injuries and said that the period of care for them might previously have been underestimated.

Again, the 'line to take' with the media was specified. Again, it was less than honest. The public were to be told that 'Regional General Managers in England have been asked to consider what preparatory measures might be needed under their plans.' At a time of great financial stringency in the NHS, when general managers were struggling to keep their spending within unrealistic limits, the section on finance was brief and gave little comfort: 'Separate guidance on finance will be issued to Regional Finance Directors'.

In January 1991 the government issued a further document, 'Gulf Contingency Planning: Dealing with the Media' to NHS public relations officers. This provided suggested answers to probable press inquiries. For example: 'How many beds are the NHS providing to deal with Gulf casualties?' Suggested answer: 'This depends on the demand. No request for specific numbers of beds has yet been made.' Untrue.

Another question: 'Won't the use of NHS hospitals for military casualties increase NHS waiting lists? What is the estimate of the impact on waiting lists/times?' Suggested answer: 'We are working with the health authorities to minimize disruption to the NHS. But depending on the numbers of casualties allocated to each hospital, there may have to be some curtailment of non-emergency admissions, although consideration will be given afterwards to how deferred NHS cases can be dealt with quickly. Emergency admissions will not be affected.'

The truth was that at that time, in January, non-urgent admissions were already being deferred, that patients were already being sent home early, that community services were already feeling the strain. This at a time when, with the imminent introduction of the White Paper changes and the upheaval of the NHS internal market, staff were already feeling vulnerable and morale was already at a low ebb. Not only 'services' were feeling the strain. Vulnerable individuals were suffering.

A further distortion of the truth in the media document: 'Can chemical contamination or biological infection be transmitted to others?' Suggested answer: 'British clinicians have built up a considerable volume of information about how to treat these cases (a number of patients from the Iran/Iraq conflict were treated in Britain) and that information is widely available.' One of the clinicians primarily involved in treating these chemical burns patients, Professor Angus McGrouther, Britain's only Professor of

Plastic and Reconstructive Surgery, said, 'At the very most, the health service would be able to treat only about 150 such casualties at one time; there are no more than thirty plastic surgery or burns units in the country, and they could handle only five patients each because of the intensive treatment required.'

A leading article in the *British Medical Journal* of 19 January 1991[2] stated: 'Our experience of war surgery is limited'. This article argued that major civilian accidents had taught us that 'Communications and the command structure and co-ordination across professional and geographical boundaries are recognized as essential ingredients of an efficient plan' and that this efficiency had been demonstrated in, for instance, the Cannon Street rail crash. The severity of wartime injuries would, however, the author stated, be much greater and there would be a heavy load of post-operative complications. In other words, the burden on the NHS would extend far beyond the duration of the war.

The media document was predictably optimistic. 'The available facilities will more than meet the number of casualties which could be referred to us in a worst-case scenario.' As this document was being distributed, London health districts were struggling to cope with the seasonal demand for beds. In one district, City and Hackney, there was, for several days, not one available bed in the entire district. Wards had been identified and closed in preparation for reception of war casualties, while elderly patients suffering from chest infections and strokes were shuffled around hospitals in an often futile search for an empty and available bed. In the year since April 1990, in London alone, over 1,000 hospital beds have been cut. Nearly 30 per cent of the admissions sought by the Emergency Bed Service, an agency which chases beds across the capital on behalf of desperate referring doctors, are refused through lack of space.

Even in peacetime, patients are denied timely treatment and are caused unnecessary suffering, because of NHS underresourcing. A sudden wartime influx of resources into the starved NHS could not magically create the full or even safe complement of nursing

staff so lacking in peacetime. Yet the media document alleged:
'The NHS contingency plans have a wide measure of flexibility
built in and a full range of skills is, of course, available.' Before the
war, wards had lain locked up and dormant because the NHS was
too poor to train nurses to staff them.

Public and press concern with this situation was recognized in
expected question number 17: 'Has the NHS sufficient capacity to
cope? Won't you need to reopen wards closed because of the NHS
financial crisis?' Suggested answer: 'Financial constraints will not
be allowed to inhibit the in-treatment of emergency patients. It will
be for health authorities to decide whether wards not currently
operational will need to be reactivated to receive casualties from
the Gulf, or whether they can secure sufficient facilities (theatres,
beds, etc.) by deferring non-urgent admissions. On a contingency
basis, some units have already asked for volunteers to stand by for
special duty should the need arise (e.g. from former staff).'

Indeed they had. General practitioners in, for example, Oxford
had been asked whether they would be prepared to leave their
patients in the community and go to work in the local hospitals. A
difficult ethical decision. No doctor easily refuses medical help to
those who need it, but no GP relishes the thought of relinquishing
his or her responsibility to their particular patients.

This sort of psychological pressure was being universally felt by
health service staff. Fear of the unknown was prevalent: of the
types and severity of injuries which would be encountered, of what
it would actually feel like to be faced with a gruesomely mutilated
human being lying in front of you – especially if, as seemed likely
at the time, victims of chemical weapons started to return. As often
in disaster situations it would be the junior staff, the young house
officers and trainee nurses, who would have first exposure to such
'cases'.

Did they feel prepared? The government chose to perpetrate the
delusion that they did; that resources, in terms of number of staff,
facilities, information and psychological support, were fully available. This is, of course, the delusion they have chosen to perpetrate

about the health service in peacetime for many years. The experience of anyone actually working in the service, on the front line, is very different.

A few examples of good practice, of health authorities anticipating and trying to respond to their staff's anxieties and need for honest information, did emerge.

City and Hackney Health Authority circulated a 'Communication to All Staff' outlining the current situation. A hundred and eighty-one beds would be available for military casualties: 'We cannot predict the nature of the casualties in the first instance, but they are unlikely to be the most serious cases as these will probably be retained in military hospitals in the Gulf.' A questionnaire had gone to all nursing staff regarding the possibility of working additional hours, and a callout system was planned: 'It will be important for staff to maintain their ability to function effectively and I would recommend that all "volunteers" have at least one day off each week.' Arrangements had been made for extended crèche facilities and a Gulf Staffing Hotline had been established to co-ordinate all staffing activities.

Exeter Health Authority distributed a circular, 'Gulf Emergency – Use of Local Hospitals,' to keep staff informed and involved.

In Oxfordshire, the Mental Health Unit and social services had collaborated to form the Oxfordshire Gulf War Psychosocial Support Group. They produced a document, 'Advice for Caring for Victims and their Relatives', which described common feelings and reactions of casualties (fear, grief, shame, guilt, anger, denial, numbing, repeated memories and nightmares) and of relatives. It outlined the reactions which staff themselves might expect to suffer – helplessness, feeling incompetent or deskilled, sadness, conflict, anger, guilt, sleep disturbance, excessive smoking and drinking – and gave suggestions about how to cope. The importance of adequate rest and expression of feelings was emphasized.

The Medical Campaign Against Nuclear Weapons (MCANW), an organization of health workers which campaigned vigorously against going to war and then, once the war had started, for a humanitarian cease-fire,[3] initiated a network of psychologists and psychiatrists to provide a psychiatric service for casualties and counselling and support for hospital staff. They particularly drew attention to the morbidity attached to the post-traumatic disaster syndrome (PTDS) and to the high suicide rate, as occurred after Vietnam, if proper support was not provided. This network attracted disparaging comment from Ministry of Defence psychiatrists who alleged that they had already made adequate provision.

A meeting of two hundred mental health professionals held by the Medical Campaign, just before the onset of war, had produced a statement which had predicted that any victory would be pyrrhic and that the whole world would suffer. It had described how the rush to war was being driven by irrational psychological processes, including the denial of reality when it becomes too painful to face, the obsession with secrecy, individual leaders' needs for personal power, aggressive impulses being recognized in others but not in one's own self or group, the search for an external 'enemy' to distract attention from internal problems, the appeal of the delusion of 'winning' a war, the extreme difficulty of bearing uncertainty, particularly over time.

Whether or not senior government officials recognized these processes in themselves, they continued to be driven by them, and British forces went to war a few days later.

The government's lack of understanding of human psychology and psychiatry was further demonstrated in the 'Dealing with the Media' document. The suggested answer to the question 'Will psychiatric services in the NHS be available to treat returning military personnel and are there sufficient resources to cope?' was, somewhat briefly and very optimistically: 'The NHS will provide the services which are needed'. This glibly denied the psychological trauma to which military personnel might be subjected in such a war. As it turned out, of course, the expected strain, thankfully, was not imposed on the NHS psychiatric services.

How could NHS staff have faith in a government which broke

the basic rules of good planning, which was intent on being dishonest to them and the public about the likely consequences of war in the Gulf? Responding to the media document, the Medical Campaign issued a position statement:

> MCANW supports all NHS and military staff in their treatment of casualties from the Gulf War. MCANW wishes for efficient NHS planning and adequate resourcing in order to optimize the treatment of Gulf casualties and of the NHS' existing patients. This requires the provision of full and accurate information to medical personnel, press and public alike.

In other words, the government should be honest. In the months before the war, when the Medical Campaign was publicizing the probable consequences of a Gulf War based on predictions from the Center for Defense Information in Washington (not an institution known for wild exaggeration), its members were often accused of being alarmist. Not alarmist but honest, they said.

After the war had started, the Medical Campaign circulated a petition throughout hospitals, surgeries and health centres to give individuals an opportunity to state their opposition to the war, to urge its early conclusion and to publicize its effects on the NHS. It aimed to promote sincere discussion in the NHS on the issues surrounding the war and to help individuals overcome the sense of frustration and powerlessness which put them at risk of psychological morbidity and depression. The petition, signed by such eminent people as Sir Raymond Hoffenburg, ex-President of the Royal College of Physicians, Dr Sheila Adam, Regional Director of Public Health, North West Thames Regional Authority, and Anton Obholzer, chair of the Tavistock Clinic, was delivered to the Prime Minister on 19 February 1991 and attracted a lot of general and medical press attention.

By that time, the public were beginning to be aware that there was another side to the government's propaganda coin – that the war might not be a Falklands-type exercise, fought in a country a long way away without, in any substantial way, impinging on the health service and the quality of life at home.

For NHS staff, pressures were increasing. Junior medical staff in central London teaching hospitals were having their annual leave cancelled. There were beds and wards still lying empty, while waiting lists lengthened. Fax machines were appearing in hospital offices with strict instructions that they were not to be used for anything other than 'Gulf business'.

In the aftermath of the crisis, what will become of the fax machines? Will wards opened for military sick stay open for civilian sick? Will the information technology given an airing during the crisis be able to cope with the demands imposed on it by the government's 'reforms' of the NHS, the new system of internal trading?

Since its inception ten years ago the Medical Campaign has struggled to make colleagues and the public aware that money spent on war or preparation for war is money that could otherwise be spent on health. The comparisons are familiar . . . one Trident submarine (£1 billion) would buy a five-year universal child immunization programme with a million lives saved; one nuclear test would buy training for 40,000 health workers in Africa; global arms spending per minute would buy 5,000 clean-water wells and pumps for the Third World, or 500 primary schools in Latin America, or 5,500 NHS nursing sisters for one year, or 4,000 hip replacement operations on the NHS, or 100 kidney machines for the NHS.

The Gulf War made such comparisons even more pungent. The expense of the UK's contribution to the Gulf action was some £3 million per day. The UK government's entire 1990 allocation to African famine relief was £7.2 million, about two and a half days' worth of being in the Gulf . . . As the government was pursuing its hugely expensive course in the Gulf, it was being estimated that 27 million people in Africa were at risk of dying from starvation. What did the UK government see fit to give? A paltry £20 million – about six days' worth of war.

The total costs of the war, in terms of human suffering and environmental degradation, are incalculable. The language used attempted to minimize the emotional impact – targets, war machine, collateral . . . rarely people. An estimated 100,000 Iraqi soldiers were killed. The number of civilians killed is unknown. With the awful damage to the country's infrastructure, disastrous epidemics of malnutrition and infectious diseases such as cholera and typhoid are inevitable. Stocks of antibiotics are very low, anaesthetics are nonexistent, treatments and drugs for cancer and renal failure patients are not available.

In the aftermath of the war there is a crucial question which must be asked of the UK government: to what extent will they provide a medical response to the Middle East public health catastrophe which they helped to create? We must hope that they will now show more honesty and integrity than they showed before and during the war.

## Notes

1. 'Gulf Contingency Planning – NHS Plan and Procedure Guide (Operation Granby)', Department of Health, 14 December 1990.

2. David W. Yates, 'The NHS prepares for war. There should be lessons for peacetime', *British Medical Journal*, 1991; 302:130.

3. Medical Campaign Against Nuclear Weapons, 601 Holloway Road, London N19 5DG. Tel. 071-272 2020.

# ABBAS SHIBLAK

## *The Deepening Tragedy of the Palestinians*

After the invasion of Kuwait and the war that followed, Palestinians in Britain, like other Palestinian communities in the diaspora, spent months of agonized uncertainty over the fate of their loved ones and friends in Kuwait. 'It was worse than 1948,' one said. 'We lost our country then; now we are still without a country but we have been starved, rejected and discriminated against by our fellow Arabs. Since 1948, we have been building other people's homes but not our own.'

Nearly half a million Palestinians were living in Kuwait when the Iraqi invasion took place. They were mostly there to make a living, since the heady days for making money of the early 1950s and 1960s. All this is over for most of them. They live from hand to mouth, spending what they can get. They are in Kuwait because they were offered a job, which is more and more difficult for them to find anywhere else. The Palestinians, like other foreigners in Kuwait, are not allowed to own property or shares, or to conduct a business without being in partnership with a Kuwaiti national.

Since the late 1970s, in fact, any prospect of work for the Palestinians has become very slim, if not impossible. Those who reach the age of twenty-one and have no work have to leave the country without their families, even if they were born in Kuwait or have no valid visa to any other country. In recent years even Palestinians who have spent more than thirty or forty years in the country have found it more and more difficult to acquire visit visas to their parents or their children.

These Palestinians are part of a nation of five million. Two million live in historic Palestine (1.5 in the West Bank and Gaza, 0.5 in Israel) and three million in the diaspora mainly in the surrounding Arab countries, but an increasing number have settled overseas in America, Europe and Australia. Those who live in Arab countries are subjected to various forms of discrimination in breach of successive resolutions taken by the League of Arab States to treat them equally with their own nationals, and also in breach of the International Code on refugee status. In Egypt, for instance, Palestinians have never had their documentation properly recognized, but need to have a visa somewhere else in order to be allowed to stay in Egypt. In Lebanon there are different laws for Palestinians as opposed to other people and they are excluded from certain jobs, while in the Mahgreb entry for Palestinians is restricted, and in Saudi Arabia and some of the Gulf states not allowed at all. With the advance of the Palestinian National Movement (PNM) since the late 1960s, the high political profile of the Palestinians has attracted more suspicion, uncertainty and persecution towards them, especially those communities in demographically fragile and delicately balanced societies like Jordan, Lebanon and Kuwait.

In fact, in the case of Kuwait, the number of Palestinians almost equalled the number of original Kuwaitis. In the 1970s the common names for the Palestinian quarters in Kuwait – Al-Nugra and Al-Hawali – were changed to new ones, 'Sabra' and 'Shatilla', which indicate implicitly the militant character of these quarters, similar to those of the camps of Lebanon. At the time, Kuwait was developing chronic fears for its own stability from developments in three neighbouring countries: Iran, Iraq and Syria. In fact Islamic fundamentalists almost succeeded in killing the Emir in 1985.

The Palestinians' misfortune is that they lost their country at the time when everyone else was getting their own. The disintegration of the Arab East, as part of the colonial scheme which began at the turn of the century, was already under way. The social and economic transformation which followed – the impact of the tremendous, yet inequitable, wealth brought about by the oil and the absence of any democracy and political freedom – helped this process and led to the eventual failure of pan-Arab nationalism. The minority ruling elites – whether tribal, military or a mixture of both – in most Arab countries pursued narrow nationalistic policies to remain in power.

The Palestinians were thus left out in the cold: the untouchables – orphans among the spoilt children of an affluent generation. The dilemma of the PNM today is that it is growing up in the diaspora in a hostile environment where Arab society is little changed from the social and political scene of the undemocratic days of 1948. Although the Palestine Liberation Organization (PLO) is a member of the League of Arab States, it has no state of autonomy of its own and was never accepted on equal terms. In essence, it is a popular movement which is largely in contradiction, in nature and objectives, with the official Arab position. Yet for reasons beyond the scope of this chapter, it falls short of being transformed into the mass Arab popular movement which its very survival needs. It therefore, remains vulnerable to pressure, attempts at containment and physical liquidation – such as in Jordan in 1970–1, the massacres in Lebanon in 1982, and individual targeting like the recent assassination in Tunis of Abu Iyad and two other PLO officials.

The Ba'athists in Syria and Iraq tried to control the movement through direct threat and crude intervention. They created their own factions within the movement which in fact served their manipulators' purposes, not the Palestinian cause. The wealthy Gulf States used their wealth to influence the movement, to marginalize it and to channel their backing to its opponents when it suited them. It is no longer a secret that when Israel launched its savage invasion of Lebanon in 1982 to finish off the PLO, Arab governments were told in advance.

Palestine, for Arabs and Muslims alike, is a just and popular cause. For their governments it is a burden, a time bomb which threatens some of their fundamental weaknesses. The only thing they can afford to do, therefore, is to give it their vocal support, often in the most aggressive manner to suit their domestic needs, while suppressing any move to restore Palestinian rights or to make a just and durable peace nearer or more achievable. It is quite normal, in Arab diplomatic circles, for an Emir in one of the Gulf States to visit a cousin ruler in another State overnight for a personal matter, such as to present him with a racing camel, and a communiqué is issued the next morning stating that the two rulers discussed the Palestinian question. Saddam Hussein's behaviour over Kuwait is a striking example of manipulation of the Palestinian cause by Arab officials. He inflicted grave and strategic damage to the Palestinian cause by trying to undermine the PLO's peaceful and realistic manifesto in the mid 1970s, by starting the war with Iran and by his dismissal of all attempts at reconciliation with Syria.

It was the Egyptian President Gamal Abdel Nasser who, in private discussion in 1967, gave the Palestinians the most honest statement from an Arab leader: 'Don't ever believe that any Arab leader, including myself, has any plan to liberate Palestine,' he said. These thoughts were the background to his setting up the PLO – as a weak and hollow framework intended to control the militancy that was just beginning.

It was only after the Israeli occupation of Arab territories (Golan and Sinai) in 1967 that Egypt and Syria started a war against Israel with the specific objectives of regaining the occupied areas. One always thinks how groundless and misleading is the Zionist claim that Israel is facing one hundred million Arabs of twenty-one armies, and how the official Arab rhetoric often helps Israel in this sense. It is the Palestinians whose security was grossly breached, whose development and democratic rights were savagely halted. It is they who are in real need of peace and security.

Two recent historical events have special significance for the Palestinians; the first is that the PNM took over the PLO in 1968 and enforced *de facto* recognition from the Arab states in a moment of defeat and humiliation imposed upon them, following the 1967 war. It took the Arab states another six years – not without effort – to recognize the PLO as the only legitimate representative of the

Palestinians in the Al-Rabat Summit of 1974. The second was when the Arab states, in the Amman Summit of 1988, saw an attempt made to marginalize the Palestinian cause and to revoke the right of the PLO on the issue of representation. In an instinctive response the Palestinians in the occupied territories rose in a spectacular show of defiance, demanding the end of the occupation, freedom in a sovereign state of their own and support for the PLO. The *intifada* started and the PNM entered a new era which gives more emphasis to popular mobilization and peaceful means of resistance inside Palestine. The *intifada* gave the movement the new blood it needs to stand up to the oppressive Israeli occupation inside, as well as Arab pressure outside. How ironical that those who are under the occupation embrace the bruised, butchered movement in exile, which has suffered at the hands of Arab governments more than it has suffered from the Israelis!

For those Palestinians living under the subjugation of the Israeli occupation, as well as those who are living in deprivation, dispossession and daily humiliation in exile, the Palestinian homeland became in fact a human as well as a political ideological necessity. For the Palestinians, the Palestinian homeland is seen not only as a fulfilment of their legitimate right for self-determination *vis-à-vis* the Zionist scheme, but also as a natural outcome of the developments which have taken place in the Arab region over the last five or six decades. Recent years have seen the failure of Pan-Arab nationalist ideology as the ruling elites have clung to colonial boundaries. Increasingly the Palestinians, thirty years ago the most active element in Arab ideology, do not fit into the new preoccupation. The Palestinians are a nation which was kept in waiting for too long. The manipulation, the sadistic mistreatment and the campaign of discredit to which they were subjected during the Gulf War highlighted this with stunning urgency.

The Palestinians' views on the Gulf crisis were seen largely through an arbitrary and oversimplified American system of sorting out

various views during the crisis. The world was suddenly divided
into two camps: those 'pro' Saddam Hussein and those opposed to
him. The world was returned to the era of the late John Foster
Dulles. There was no place for neutrality or compromise. The
American Administration assumed the role of custodian of world
morality. Small countries – some with a long-standing pro-Western
attitude, like Tunisia, Jordan and Yemen – were harshly penalized
simply for not joining the American-led coalition forces in the
Gulf.

The official PLO position – from the first proposal it made to
the last – was to uphold the principle of withdrawal of Iraqi forces
from Kuwait, to avoid foreign intervention and to find a peaceful
solution within a regional – primarily Arab – formula. It adheres to
the need to apply international legitimacy in all disputes. The
Palestinian leadership were actively involved in trying to limit the
damage and then to secure an early Arab solution. But these
efforts, and others, were contemptuously brushed aside by the
Americans.

To achieve a fair assessment of the Palestinian position, therefore, one must consider some basic facts:

a. The early American intervention altered the debate in Arab
   and Muslim circles to a large extent from the Iraqi invasion,
   which many saw as an internal Arab matter, to a more urgent
   and far more dangerous issue: how to avoid a destructive war
   over which the Arabs would have no control. Fears and
   suspicions, which have historical justification because of
   Western domination, started to gain ground. The Americans
   were seen as out to reassert Western control of Arab destinies
   and resources. The sins of Saddam Hussein, who was the
   first to be blamed for provoking this hurricane, were easily
   overlooked.
b. The Americans' failure to show the same strength of feeling
   towards Palestine as they did towards Kuwait was another
   factor which influenced the views of many Arabs, and the

Palestinians in particular. It was widely and legitimately argued: Why did the Americans never contemplate similar action to counter twenty-three years of Israeli occupation of Arab lands? For those Arabs, the duplicity and the hypocrisy of the West were so blatant that all claims to morality in liberating Kuwait by the American-led coalition seemed a mockery. The views of the majority of Arabs, the Palestinians included, were in the final analysis a sign of defiance and rejection of the US intervention more than support for Saddam Hussein or complacency about the fate of Kuwait.

The position taken by the Palestinian leadership reflected this very clearly. They were in harmony with the popular mood among the Arabs and the Palestinian masses and in harmony with the PLO as a liberation movement which could never give its blessng to American military intervention. Some rhetoric and vocal support for Iraq from Yasser Arafat during the crisis was highlighted, often distorted and exploited to discredit the PLO. The Israelis and the Americans were quick to claim that the Palestinian leadership damaged their political credibility and their international standing by 'supporting Saddam Hussein'. The PLO should not therefore be considered an acceptable partner in any peace negotiation.

But this was the view of the Israelis and the Americans all along, well before the Gulf crisis. They are the only countries – apart, perhaps, from South Africa – who still refuse to recognize the PLO and the Palestinian right to self-determination. New excuses thus need to be devised for the old policies.

The PLO is the only available framework for the Palestinians in their march to achieve their national rights, and it symbolizes their aspiration to live in a free and independent state of their own. The PLO embraces representatives of all: politically active groups, communities inside Palestine and the diaspora, trade unions and independent activist and public figures. The leadership are democratically elected by the Palestinian National Council (PNC) or the Palestinian Parliament.

It is only for the Palestinians themselves to decide who is going to represent them and to speak on their behalf. They are no longer invisible, nor do they need to be cared for by any of the Arab governments. One of the favourite slogans for which the Palestinians paid with their blood is: 'No to guardianship, No to occupation'. As the Israeli occupation continues, the Palestinians see the termination of Arab governments' guardianship as their main, if not their only, achivement in the last twenty-five years. Any attempt to overlook this would be as futile as trying to put a genie back in a bottle, and would have far-reaching destabilizing effects on the region as a whole.

The real Palestinian tragedy seems to be that their right to statehood, to freedom from oppression and occupation is conditional on their good behaviour. If they are found wanting by 'supporting Saddam Hussein', then their rights can be called into question by Western leaders who are quite ready to support undemocratic, feudal and brutal regimes in the Middle East, and all over the world, if it suits their strategic book.


How can one describe American behaviour when this Administration opened the post-Cold War era with its invasion of Panama, imposing the rule of the 10 per cent white minority and guaranteeing US control over the Canal and the bases that have been used to train various gangster groups who terrorize Latin America?

How can one also describe the behaviour of the Americans' client in the Middle East – Israel's harsh occupation, its savage treatment and daily killings of the Palestinians, its refusal to honour the Security Council resolutions on the Palestinian question, or Israeli co-operation with the apartheid regime in South Africa and its arms supplies to the most ruthless dictatorships in Latin America? Plainly, the Americans have no moral grounds for questioning the Palestinians' behaviour. The Palestinians, in the end, are the victims of the Americans' unequivocal support to Israel and the US/Israeli responsibility for the numerous foiled peace efforts.

In fact, the question which is more relevant and needs to be asked here is: where do the two sides, the Palestinians and the Israelis, stand on the main principles, which are universally admitted, for a peaceful settlement in the Middle East? The Palestinian position still advocates peaceful settlement based on Israeli withdrawal from the occupied territories of 1967 and the two-state solution. This was originally endorsed in the PNC meeting of 1974 and later illustrated in clearer terms in the 'Peace Initiative' endorsed in the PNC meeting in Algeria in 1988.

In December the same year, at a special Geneva session of the UN, Yasser Arafat told the world that the two-state solution involving the Palestinian renunciation of 77 per cent of their original homeland was the Palestinians' goal. Arafat accepted Security Council Resolution 242 and recognized Israel's right to exist. He reiterated this position recently during the Gulf crisis and resumed his peace offensive after the war by offering the PLO acceptance of a UN buffer zone on the border with Israel, Jewish members in the Palestinian Cabinet, and Jewish citizens of the Palestinian state. He showed flexibility on territories if the Israelis agreed to do the same. The PLO dismissed all along any suggestion that the *intifada* should develop from a community-based peaceful show of resistance and stone-throwing to armed insurrection. It asserted too that the dialogue with the Israeli peace groups should continue.

In contrast, the official Israeli position has steadily shifted over the last decade to become more intransigent. The Israeli government has not accepted the principle of withdrawal to 1967 borders as required by Security Council Resolutions 242 and 338. Israel officially annexed East Jerusalem and the Golan Heights and is still occupying large areas in Southern Lebanon, refusing to implement Security Council Resolution 425. Israel is still adamant about not talking to the PLO, banning any contacts with it and refusing to recognize the Palestinian people's right to self-determination. Israel pursued its harsh policies unchallenged in the occupied territories: annexing Arab land; building new settlements; subjecting people to barbaric and murderous measures of torture, imprisonment and daily killings; applying collective punishments: starvation and economic destruction.

One might ask those in the West who expend so much energy on making sure that the Palestinians are 'well-behaved': how can they lose sight of a simple fact – that peace needs two sides, and Israel has not shown its readiness to be one? Those who hurried to reward Israel for its stand during the Gulf crisis were in fact giving Shamir's government new ammunition to be more stubborn and more intransigent – at least this is how the Likud government understood the message. While the world was busy with the Gulf, Shamir clung to his hardline position, building blockades ahead of any possible efforts to secure lasting settlement in the aftermath of the Gulf War.

Undoubtedly, the USA found itself in a unique and commanding position with the end of the Cold War, but it is a position won with great ferocity. The influence of the Soviet Union on the global scene has been drastically marginalized. The threat of the pre-eminence of Japanese economic power has been successfully checked. The Europeans failed to present any coherent policies not in complete agreement with the US line. Whether they will be more prepared to pursue a more independent line after the war is still unclear.

History, however, shows that military might can bring about a successful war but not a successful political settlement. The failure of the Soviet Union in Afghanistan and that of Israel in the Middle East are but two examples.

Washington's ambitious postwar agenda includes four objectives: regional arrangements in the Gulf for security, economic co-operation, arms control and a resolution of the Arab–Israeli conflict. The US Administration may be sincere in its determination to move speedily to achieve these goals given the global role it has assumed during the crisis and the need to sustain its credibility. The question is: will the USA be able to put forward effective formulas before the Middle East witnesses another upheaval?

The Palestinian question is the keystone to the postwar settlement, affecting the prospect of stability, peace and arms control, regionally and globally as well. The Israeli intransigence and the blank-cheque policy of support it had and still enjoys from the USA remains the main obstacle to any peaceful solution. Peaceful experience proves that peace in the Middle East needs a radical change of attitude and fresh thinking from the American side. If the USA sticks to some of its old doctrines, it is doubtful that the new effort will be able to bring any lasting peace.

So far, the American proposals do not go beyond a vague formulation, but disturbing signals have begun to emerge indicating the desire to apply some old and unworkable remedies. The new element here is perhaps that the Americans – inspired, of course, by their global commanding role and their military success in the Gulf War – feel more than ever the will and the capability to impose their own order. These signals are related, at least, to three essential elements in any peaceful settlement of the Arab–Israeli conflict.

First: there is a desire on the part of the Americans to deny the UN the instrumental role it is supposed to assume in building the peace in accordance with successive UN resolutions. Obviously, the organization cannot be manipulated in this case, as it was in the conduct of the Gulf War. Contrary to Arab and European wishes for an international peace conference, the Americans are now pushing towards direct and separate negotiations under their auspices. This would be a revived and reshaped Camp David process. They see only a ceremonial role for the UN, the Europeans or the Soviet Union.

Second: confronted with stubbornness and blackmail from the Israeli side and fear and submission from the Arab side, the US

Administration seems more willing to put pressure on Arab states for more concessions. It sustains the old approach, which proved unworkable in the past: that Israel will come to its senses by persuasion and not by pressure. More financial aid was pumped in during the Gulf crisis over and above the present amount, running in recent years at the rate of 3.5 billion dollars annually, or 10 million dollars a day. Some recent reports have referred to a $20 billion grand scheme to pump water from Turkey to Israel which the Americans seem to have discussed during the trip made by James Baker to the region directly after the war in the Gulf. Such a scheme could mean the physical transformation of the region – one which would allow Israel to absorb thousands more Soviet immigrants. It would also, of course, further cripple the industrial and agricultural potential of Iraq by this diversion of its water resources. Israel was also assured that it can keep its arsenal of nuclear, chemical and other weapons of mass destruction, while the Arabs should be stripped of any capabilities to have or to produce such weapons in the future.

Third: the Americans seem to be trapped with their old policies towards the Palestinians – No to the PLO, No to the Palestinian state – and still entertaining schemes which fall short of full implementation of the Palestinians' right of self-determination, including the right to have a free and independent state of their own. American efforts seem to focus on ending the state of war between the Arab states and Israel and addressing the Palestinian question in a very nominal way. They are in favour of a 'twin-track' approach; parallel Arab–Israeli and Palestinian–Israeli negotiations.

The Americans will be deceiving themselves if they think that any Arab state, including those who are now after Arafat's head, can be swept away by the postwar euphoria into signing a new Camp David-style accord which overlooks the Palestinians' legitimate rights. Some Arab states, including the Gulf States, have expressed unease about going to a regional conference, proposed by the USA, aimed at ending their conflict with Israel without a clear and decisive formula on how to tackle the Palestinian question. Neither will the USA be able to find an alternative to the PLO ready to make, on behalf of the Palestinians, concessions which exceed the peace initiative endorsed by the PNC in 1988.

With the present US attitudes towards the PLO, Israel's continuous refusal to budge and the fear of most Arab governments in the American-led coalition to undermine their standing at home further, peace remains as remote as ever. One track of the 'twin-track' approach, the Palestinian–Israeli negotiation, will prove to be blocked, while the other, the Arab–Israeli negotiation, will not achieve much.

In the aftermath of the war, the USA's 'new world order' for the Palestinians is becoming clearer, according to commentators with inside sources. The solution was outlined by James Baker well before the Gulf crisis: Jordan is the Palestinian state; the occupied territories are to be ruled according to the basic guidelines of the Israeli government which would give them handicapped or limited administrative autonomy; their political representatives will be chosen for them, with the PLO excluded; and 'free elections' will be held under Israeli military control, with the Palestinian leadership either in prison or deported. The Israelis will be hailed as generous and forthcoming.

The sufferings of the Palestinians in the diaspora, like those of Kuwait, will be intensified. They will be subjected to more manipulation, deprivation and political suppression at the hands of the tribal and unpopular host Arab governments, spurred on by a mixture of fear of disloyalty and the desire to please their American masters. They will be denied access to proper education, work or free movement and the right to bring up their children in a safe and secure haven of their choice. Their personal safety and their cause will continue to be the first casualty of the absense of democracy in the region.

As for those who are living under the Israeli occupation, they have had no chance of any economic development while their land

and water were taken away. They have been permitted to serve the Israeli economy as virtual slave labour. The recent curfew imposed in the West Bank by the Israelis during the Gulf War was a further blow to the livelihood of the Palestinians.

The victors in the Gulf War can now proceed with the policy articulated in February 1989 by Yitzhak Rabin of the Israeli Labour Party, then Defence Minister, when he told Peace Now leaders of his satisfaction with the USA–PLO dialogue: 'meaningless discussions to divert attention while Israel suppresses the *intifada* by force'. Rabin promised: 'the Palestinians will be broken', reiterating the prediction of Israeli Arabists forty years earlier: 'They will be crushed, turned into human dust and the waste of society, and join the most impoverished classes in the Arab countries.' Or they will leave, while Russian Jews, who are effectively barred from the USA by Washington's policies designed to deny them a free choice of where they settle, flock to an expanded Israel.

The war in the Gulf might have opened the Middle East to new promises and potentialities as the Americans see it, but most Arabs, and Palestinians in particular, see further turbulence and destabilization to come. If the Americans move to impose their own order, they will have to stay to keep it. There is enough evidence, then, to foresee what path the region is going to take, given the postwar combination: devastated economies, more direct Western control, paralysed Arab co-ordination and failure to solve chronic disputes – above all the Palestinian problem – in a just and comprehensive manner.

# JOHN VIDAL

## *Poisoned Sand and Seas*

The cormorant bird stood still. Mute. Hopeless. Slowly dying on a long white beach lapped ever so gently by a tar-black sea stretching to the horizon. In what until then had been a depersonalized video war played out on the computer screens of Tornadoes, where smart bombs destroyed only property and life supposedly went on regardless, that wretched bird on the beach near Khafji became the first symbol of death for the West and the first confirmation that the environment, the very foundation of human well-being, would be a major casualty of this war.

A fortnight later, acrid, poisonous cliffs of smoke from the oil fires in Kuwait were billowing two miles high, 400 miles south and 60 miles east and west. Black, oily rain was falling in Turkey, Iran and later the Himalayas. In the noonday darkness of a ravished city, temperatures were 15 degrees (centigrade) below average and the choking photochemical smog was far worse than in Mexico City in high summer. The very resource the Western Allies were fighting for to drive its industrial machine was being destroyed before its eyes. The irony was lost in the smoke.

Three more weeks, and Iraq was found to be paralysed. Everything that would normally sustain life was breaking down. The theatre of war has many parts: now cholera and typhoid stood in the wings, and famine – all but forgotten just a few hundred miles south-west in the Red Sea Hills of Sudan – rehearsed its lines. In Baghdad, thousands had taken to drawing water from the polluted Tigris or puddles in the street; the sewers were blocked, the water purification plants useless, the hospitals powerless. What, just six months before, was one of the healthiest cities in the Middle East, with more hospitals per inhabitant than London, was now a cradle of disease and pestilence. And in the rich, fertile countryside south of Baghdad, where B-52s had pounded the land for weeks, the intricate, ancient irrigation systems lay shattered, abandoned and polluted. The full devastation of life for 18 million people in Iraq remains to be seen.

Water, air, earth, fire: war is elemental, and never more so than this one. In a fight for the security of one resource, every other resource known to humankind was employed to wreak massive destruction on people's way of life. Yet for all the justification given for combat, the possible environmental consequences were wilfully ignored by the United Nations, the European Community, all participating governments and the oil industry, before and during the conflict. Even though Saddam Hussein had warned the West in October 1990 that he would set fire to the wells and create and light 'a sea of oil', and the industry knew that he had mined the wellheads, the forces of government chose not to listen. Nature, it was implied by the silence which greeted his threats, would not be harmed, or would recover. Nature had no part in the events. Nature had nothing to do with war or people's lives. Nature would have nothing to do with the reconstruction of the region after the war.

Even a glance at history would have shown that the environmental terrorism that humans have long waged against the environment is deeply intensified in war and infinitely complicates the stabilization of countries afterwards. Between 1961 and 1971 the Americans laid chemical waste to the forests of Vietnam. More than 55,000 tonnes of herbicides devastated hundreds of thousands of acres and a whole generation. Today, blackened tree stumps stand in useless land pockmarked by craters. The British used pesticides against the Communists in Malaysia to restrict food supplies, as did the Italians in Abyssinia (now Ethiopia). The Japanese tried, but failed, to set fire to the oilfields of Brunei.

In a 'surgical' 'turkey shoot' of a war – which, the world was told, would be over quickly – it was politically imperative to keep the environment and other long-term considerations out of the discussions. Those who raised the environmental potential for disaster were simply ignored or dismissed. King Husain of Jordan became an early casualty, playing his environmental court card in mid-November 1990. His scientists, he said, estimated that if half of Kuwait's oil reserves (some 50 billion barrels) were to go up in flames, the impact would be devastating. Emissions of carbon monoxide and sulphur dioxide would surpass internationally accepted standards by 'factors of hundreds' and would blacken the skies over a radius of at least 750 kilometres from Kuwait. Massive carbon dioxide emissions, he said, would promote the Greenhouse Effect and contribute to global warming, climate changes and human and animal health deterioration. The environmental and human toll would 'be beyond our wildest fears'. It was the doomsday scenario.

It was also a political card, played to try and prevent the war which he knew would devastate and divide the region, but in many respects, as we shall see, King Husain was not far wrong. In Britain, the Department of the Environment dismissed his speech, said his fears for climate change and global warming were 'a red herring' and went back to the poll tax. But King Husain had jolted independent climate-modellers and atmospheric scientists. Within days their computers were churning out forecasts. From Germany came predictions that monsoon patterns would be shifted, affecting millions in the Indian subcontinent. A sort of scientific consensus was reached at a meeting in London just after Christmas from the rapidly convened War Environmental Impact Committee, made up of some of the world's leading scientists and climate-modellers who echoed many of King Husain's fears about the effects of smoke and pollution on a regional scale but dismissed the greater global warming fears. From America there was silence.

John Wakeham, the UK Energy Secretary, this time dismissed the reports as 'misleading', saying that there was no way that Kuwaiti oil reserves could disappear in one conflagration, which was less than helpful because no one then was saying that. Two weeks later the Cabinet Office issued a Meteorological Office statement which exactly mirrored the scientists claims. It said that 2.5 million tonnes of acid gases could be generated, and smoke and gas from burning wells could raise concentrations of toxic ozone at ground level and reduce levels at high altitudes. It added that such effects would be short-lived. Most embarrassingly for the British government, the Meteorological Office, in the last days of the phoney peace before 15 January 1991, agreed that the greatest environmental threat came from the smoke, which would lower ground temperatures significantly, could reduce rainfall over parts of South-East Asia during the summer monsoon, and might send some 500,000 tonnes of soot into the atmosphere.

And so, as the air war started, the environment was on the agenda, if only in the 'any other business' category. Within a week of hostilities the scientists' fears were being confirmed with every sortie. General Colin Powell, chairman of the US Chiefs of Staff, announced matter-of-factly on 23 January that bombing raids had completely destroyed two Iraqi nuclear reactors. The International Atomic Energy Authority responded that they were only research establishments and there was no danger of another Chernobyl: 'but if the reactors have been fractured there is a possibility of radioactive spillage and release into the atmosphere'. The two plants were reportedly about 5,000–8,000 kilowatts and scientists agreed that the effects would be about one three-hundredth of the scale of Chernobyl, which destroyed an area of 5,000 square kilometres and killed or affected hundreds of thousands. No details were given and no one has yet been able to analyse the immediate or long-term effects there or near the chemical weapon and nerve gas factory destroyed in the first few days at Samarra, 60 miles north of Baghdad. If the stockpiles of munitions were hit, it is certain that the fallout would have entered watercourses above and below ground, and so contaminated the food cycle.

On Tuesday 21 January 1991 the Allies attacked Iraqi tankers in the Gulf. Five supertankers, each capable of holding 100,000 tonnes of crude – no one will say how laden they were – were moored at offshore terminals. Two-mile-wide oil slicks were reported off Khafji, and sometime between then and 25 January the oil terminal at Mina Al Ahmadi was destroyed. Then – the timing is uncertain – the Iraqis opened the pumps and millions of gallons of crude poured into the Gulf from the Al Hamaji terminal.

Whether the Allies caused more oil to be spilt into the Gulf than the Iraqis may never be known, but for a few days it became politically expedient to condemn Saddam Hussein's ecological aggression and take the sting out of any accusations that the Allies were using similar tactics in their 100,000 sorties into Iraq. The media, starved of images of death, turned to filming cormorants, albeit dying in oil spilt in Allied raids. The Americans bombed the main source of oil gushing into the Gulf and largely stemmed the flow. Two months later more than 5,000 gallons of oil a day were still reported to be leaking out. Meanwhile the Saudis declared an 'ecological catastrophe' and reported that up to 11 million barrels of oil (about 460 million gallons) had escaped into the shallow Gulf, making it 'the worst oil spill in history'.

Certainly the Gulf was dreadfully polluted during the war, but it is forgotten that these waters were some of the most threatened even before the conflict. An almost enclosed sea which renews its waters only every thirty years, it is nowhere near as biologically diverse as the Red Sea or the Indian Ocean. There are rich coral islands, and the wide mudflats which stretch for hundreds of miles south towards Bahrain are home and breeding-ground to great numbers of wading birds, turtles and sea mammals. There is also a thriving shrimp and a declining fishing industry on which thousands still depend.

But oil spillages and chemical seepage from refineries and desalination plants in the Gulf are common, as is the regular dumping of toxic industrial wastes from ships. The vast landfill and dredging operations along the coast of Kuwait and Saudi Arabia have, over the years, been just as disastrous to the Gulf as oil spills. It is estimated that only 40 per cent of the Saudi coastline has not been built on in the last twenty years, reducing surface drainage from the land, lowering the water table and blocking underground fresh-water streams. The fishing industry, which once employed whole communities, is a fraction of its former size as development and oil money have moved in.

Besides, it was never the worst spill in history. Even though a third major spill reportedly developed in the north of the Gulf, within a fortnight – coincidentally, as the conservation charities flocked in with their toothbrushes and detergents behind the United Nations Environment Programme – the Saudis were rapidly revising down their estimates of the damage. First it was 8 million barrels, then 5, then 3.5. That's still enormous, but only just less than the oil spilt when the *Nowruz* oil rig was hit in the Iran–Iraq War. If the Saudis magnified the size of the spill to start with, it should be said in their defence that the military never allowed access to the spills and did not release vital environmental information which was of no military significance.

Twenty thousand birds did die, and other migratory ones will perish later as they fly in for their breeding seasons, but in the long term it will have little effect on bird population. It was, though, a potent symbol of the environmental destruction wreaked in wartime and the casual deterioration of nature. By mid-March 1991, with hundreds of acres of six-inch-deep oil contained on beaches by booms and the vast offshore spills breaking up or remaining motionless, the tentative verdict on the spills was that a number of key ecological sites had been severely damaged and might never recover, and the Gulf was another step closer to irreparable damage. The desalination plants at Jubail, which provide Riyadh with fresh water, have so far escaped, but the oil has not disappeared and the clean-up operation – helped by nature, because oil is biodegradable – will take at least a year.

Meanwhile oil fires in refineries had started only hours after the air war. Satellite photographs released in March 1991 showed that the Allies' intention right from the start was to destroy the whole Iraqi petrochemical industry. Images recorded at Imperial College, London, show toxic plumes in the first week from the northern processing centres of Baiji and Kirkuk and the Al Zubayr oilfield in the south. They also show that widespread destruction of the Kuwaiti fields began at about 7.30 a.m. GMT on 21 February at the oil processing centre of Ash Shu'aybah, just before Saddam Hussein's 'No surrender' speech and some fourteen hours before Iraqi Foreign Minister Tariq Aziz arrived in Moscow to accept the Soviet peace plan. One hour later the three-week-old plume from the Al Burqan oilfield had thickened, suggesting that more wells were on fire, and by 10 a.m. a huge toxic cloud was drifting south from the Mina Al Ahmadi centre. The cloud doubled in size and grew to about 1,000 square kilometres within twenty-four hours. By that evening at least 500 Kuwaiti wells were ablaze.

Nobody had listened to Saddam Hussein back in October 1990 when he threatened to torch Kuwait or to the environmental scientists when they warned of the consequences; but now the crocodile tears flowed from the very politicians who had sanctioned the war and the public who had tacitly supported it. Estimates of how long it would take to put out the fires varied from three to six months before the ground war. It quickly became one year or two. The oil industry wrung its hands, said that it would not affect world oil production and talked of contracts worth $10 billion to put them out. The wind – the Allies' friend when it blew towards Iraq on the day of the ground offensive and certainly prevented Saddam Hussein's use of chemical weapons – now took the choking clouds where it willed. One day it was north to Baghdad, the next south to Riyadh. On 14 March the cloud grew to 50,000 square kilometres and stretched south to the Indian Ocean. Only the heat of the fires – less than expected – and the cool March weather prevented the dense mass from rising into the stratosphere and encircling the globe in a belt of destruction. Throughout February and March

1991 it stayed at about 10,000 feet. Though no one cheered it was, in a way, the best of news. But as the desert temperatures climb, the cloud will certainly rise higher. By the end of March King Husain's scientists, rubbished in November, were predicting problems as far away as Bangladesh.

If the fires continue to burn, about 3 million barrels of oil a day for a year – a total of more than one billion barrels – will be lost. This is less than 2 per cent of Kuwait's reserves, say the oil analysts, but Kuwait holds about 10 per cent of the world's reserves and the USA alone consumes about 2.5 billion barrels of oil a year. Moreover, the gases which are being burnt off may render up to 70 per cent of Kuwait's oil untappable by present methods when the fires have been extinguished. The price of extracting it will soar, leading to greater pressure being exerted to take oil from currently marginal economic regions like the Antarctic, Alaska and the Amazon. In strict economic terms the environmental price will far surpass the many billions of dollars spent on armaments.

In the short term, Kuwait has become the pollution capital of the world. The toll that the cloud will take on the millions who must live in its potential path is inestimable. How far local climatic patterns are already being affected is unknown, but the fallout of soot, acid deposition and reduced solar radiation on groundwater supplies and agriculture will certainly have serious consequences for human health, agriculture and the marine environment throughout the region. In the meantime visibility is often reduced to a few hundred yards, the mere act of breathing becomes a problem, the grass and trees of the city are dying and the cases of bronchial asthma, boils and diarrhoea mount by the day. No one knows the long-term health effects because no one was asked to study them in advance. And in the half-light of the city the inhabitants are told nothing. In a now famous statement, the Kuwaiti Minister of Health says that the pollen count is unseasonably high. In the meantime Kuwaitis must breathe the equivalent of about fifty cigarettes a day as Red Adair and teams of uncoordinated free-enterprise US firefighters on million-dollar retainers grapple with the problem of how to put out the fires. Military equipment or personnel were not being used at the end of March 1991. British warships, each with desalination plants employed for an hour or two a day and together capable of providing fresh water for more than a million people a day, lie idle as the hospitals of the city beg for water.

As Kuwait chokes its way into hasty rehabilitation, the secondary fighting in Iraq weaves a way through the rubble of the first. What no one really contemplated before the hostilities was the scale or vigour that the Allies would employ in destroying the infrastructure of Iraq. In one month more explosives were used than were used in five years of the Second World War. Television showed the smart bombs, the ones that cruised down highways and practically shook your hand before letting themselves in through the window, but satellite pictures and the first reports from inside the country after the temporary cease-fire suggest that every town and every life in Iraq was also affected. What the television pictures didn't show was that the Allies went for the root of the country's development. This was a new kind of war which understood and took advantage of the vulnerability of technological advances; a war that simply went for everything that could nourish life; that caused identical damage to the power plants, so that cannibalization to provide limited power for hospitals, air conditioning, refrigeration was impossible; that took out irrigation pipes for farming, and communications for reporting disease; in sum, it was a war which destroyed people's environments and the potential for economic activity which in turn puts massive pressure on the government.

As in Africa, so in Iraq. The ecological cycle of food shortage is repeated endlessly across the world. A way of life is attacked; people flee and become dependent on others; by the time they can return the land has suffered; the relationship between people and their environment is ruptured and recovery – never complete – is long and painful.

Back on the oil-stained beaches of Saudi Arabia, the cormorants caught in the slicks have long since died. The Gulf waters will recover most of their ability to sustain life. The oil fires will be extinguished and the clouds of choking soot and sulphur will clear to let the Kuwaitis mine their black gold again. The cities will eventually be rebuilt, more quarries will be dug and desalinated water will run again to the hospitals, which will empty of asthmatics. New orange trees and shrubs will be planted, though the genetic resources of the region which gave the world wheat and barley will have been diminished just a little more. The desert will be cratered and pockmarked for centuries, but few people go there. The urbanized Bedouin who seek desert mushrooms at weekends will trickle back if the mines are ever cleared. There will be surprises; as the vast oil lakes being formed around the wells sink into the ground, grasses will sprout in the rejuvenated, nutrient-rich earth. The migrant workers will return and more wealth will be generated to fuel more cars, more pollution, more poverty. The environment of the region will be forgotten again by the West until the next war – perhaps this time over water.

# BARBARA ROGERS

## *Wanted: A New Policy for the United Nations*

WE THE PEOPLES OF THE UNITED NATIONS DETERMINE
to save succeeding generations from the scourge of war, which
twice in our lifetime has brought untold sorrow to mankind,
and

to reaffirm faith in fundamental human rights, in the dignity
and worth of the human person, in the equal rights of men and
women and of nations large and small, and

to establish conditions under which justice and respect for the
obligations arising from treaties and other sources of
international law can be maintained, and

to promote social progress and better standards of life in larger
freedom.

AND FOR THESE ENDS
. . . to unite our strength to maintain international peace and
security, and

to ensure, by the acceptance of principles and the institution of
methods, that armed force shall not be used, save in the
common interest . . .

**A** new look at the United Nations is long overdue in Britain. If the
Gulf War has shown up the depth of the crisis in the organization
– but also the unprecedented window of opportunity that now exists

for it to become effective as a peacekeeping operation – then this may yet come to be counted as one success in the midst of the disaster which was, and is, the war itself.

## Member States Rediscover the United Nations

The Gulf War was fought in the name of the United Nations and its Security Council. But as many commentators have pointed out, the UN was effectively hijacked as a rather thin cover for United States policy, with the aid of enough other Gulf and Western countries (especially Britain) to call itself at least a coalition. In effect, Resolution 678 gave the USA and its coalition *carte blanche* to take any action it wished against Iraq, up to and including an armed attack on its forces inside its own country, and a bombardment of its cities and key economic installations affecting the whole civilian population. Such a resolution is completely against the whole purpose of the Charter, and the UN Security Council, it could be argued, was effectively persuaded by the USA and its coalition to renounce its own responsibility to deter and punish Iraq's aggression and thereby to keep the peace.

The whole episode was pivotal in terms of the United Nations as a factor in international affairs. Not since Korea and the Congo has there been such intense discussion about the UN. The whole familiar alignment of forces went haywire and the UN seemed, incredibly, on the brink of doing what it was originally set up to do: to deter or punish aggression by one state against another, using first economic and military sanctions and then, if necessary, an international peacekeeping operation. It did not happen, and one reason for the fact that it did not is that the United States does not want the UN to work as it should.

Although the USA was able to keep control over the UN during the war itself, this situation may not continue indefinitely, simply because there are too many competing interests now jostling for a say in the organization: the United Nations has been rediscovered. Never before the Gulf War had so many different countries – from different regions and different ideological groupings – tried to use the United Nations for its intended purpose of keeping the peace and resolving international disputes. There were frantic attempts to take the issue back to the Security Council during the war itself, followed by initiatives for a UN-supervised cease-fire and full peacekeeping, supervisory and rehabilitation role. This was what the UN was originally set up for in the ruins of World War II, its first task being the relief and repatriation of war-devastated areas and the millions of displaced people, refugees and former prisoners of war.

The Soviet Union, in its long and almost-successful efforts to mediate between the USA and Iraq, repeatedly tried to initiate a debate on a cease-fire resolution in the Security Council, then put the UN at the centre of its proposed settlement just before the launch of the US-led ground assault. This is the first time the Soviets have ever tried to use the UN as a peacemaking or peacekeeping organization, and contrasts starkly with their Cold War position of damage limitation at the UN – which they regarded as a US and Western creation.

France, too, put the UN Security Council at the heart of its last-ditch peace initiative immediately before the war started. Shortly after the temporary cease-fire the French then proposed that the Security Council should hold its first-ever meeting at head-of-government level to oversee arms control and regional security. As President Mitterrand put it, 'The United Nations, which authorized the use of force, has the duty to organize the return to peace.'

Many Third World countries with few enough historical reasons for trusting the organization – Cuba, Yemen, even Iran – argued strongly for a proper debate and resolution of the crisis in New York. There was a veritable barrage of peace proposals during the war itself, virtually all of them involving the UN. The most important, and perhaps the most unexpected, was Iran's proposal for a large UN buffer force to patrol the Iraq-Kuwait border (a contingency for which the UN has already drawn up detailed plans). Iran has for so long conducted an isolationist policy that its appeal to standard UN peacekeeping procedures represents an enormous breakthrough.

All these initiatives were seen off by the Americans – with perhaps crucial help from the British delegation and backed by their nominee, Javier Pérez de Cuéllar. It was almost as if the Security Council chamber, which so many countries were trying to use for its proper purpose, had become (even more than on previous such occasions) the Americans' own private property, to be used as and when they saw fit and not otherwise. For the first three crucial weeks of the war itself, the door to the chamber remained firmly closed despite repeated attempts to restart the debate which had ostensibly led to the declaration of war by the USA in the name of this international organization.

Perhaps even more outrageous than the US refusal to discuss the war has been the cavalier dismissal of proposals to make the Security Council instrumental in establishing the peace, starting with the formal cease-fire agreement. All such attempts have been pushed aside, almost contemptuously, at the behest of the USA – which has instead pushed through Resolution 686. This amounts to President Bush's surrender terms to Iraq, coupled with the US coalition's right to restart the war if Iraq does not comply. The growing unease among Third World countries at the UN's exclusion from the peace negotiations led to opposition by Cuba and abstentions by China, India and Yemen. This meant fewer supporting votes for what purported to be the 'peace' resolution than for any of the preceding resolutions up to and including permission for war.

At the time of writing, Iraq is in the grip of civil war, the most horrific repression of popular uprisings by Saddam Hussein's Revolutionary Guards – and in the grip of a savage hunger, caused largely by the imposition, in the name of the UN, of sanctions on food supplies. This is the situation which the UN was first set up to tackle, but it is being prevented from getting involved in relief, even for refugees who have managed to flee Iraq itself or for the many nationals of other countries, especially in Asia, who have been among the first victims of the confrontation.

It seems to have passed unnoticed that the Security Council resolution imposing sanctions (Resolution 661 of 6 August 1990) specifically exempted 'supplies intended strictly for medical purposes, and in humanitarian circumstances, foodstuffs . . .' There *is* no UN authority to block supplies of food and medicines. The blockade which is being enforced is simply a case of the US coalition instructing the UN Secretariat and the specialized agencies, despite the impatience of many within them to get on with the job of urgent life-saving relief work.

A genuinely international Secretariat would insist on observing UN resolutions and would obviously refuse to accept instructions from individual member states. Disaster relief work of all kinds is something the UN and its agencies can do superbly well: their best people, both at headquarters and in the field, tend to be concentrated on this kind of task. The current situation, whereby they are blocked from precisely the kind of work in Iraq and the region as a whole which would 'reaffirm faith in fundamental human rights, in the dignity and worth of the human person', as the Charter puts it, is perhaps the strongest indictment yet of UN officials' subservience not to the peoples of the United Nations but to the governments of individual member states.

## The Question of Sanctions

Economic and military sanctions are the main weapons of international pressure against an aggressor available to the UN in its stated aim of preserving the peace. The success or otherwise of any UN sanctions programme is a crucial indicator of its ability to perform its basic role of keeping the peace. The League of Nations – set up as the guarantor of peace after the First World War – foundered on its ability to take effective sanctions measures against Italy for its invasion of Abyssinia (now Ethiopia) and against Japan over China's Manchuria, immediately before World War II broke out.

Sanctions against Iraq were indeed initiated by the Security Council back in autumn 1990. They were phenomenally successful – at least according to the CIA's testimony before Congressional hearings – going beyond anything that either the League or the UN itself had ever achieved by such measures, including sanctions against the illegal regime in Rhodesia (now Zimbabwe) after UDI, and against the apartheid regime in South Africa (sanctions which the West is now falling over itself to dismantle).

Many opponents of the war here are arguing that the assault on Iraq and its occupation of Kuwait should never have happened because sanctions, given a few more months, could have been completely successful in forcing Iraq's withdrawal. What may be nearer the mark is to ask whether perhaps it all happened so fast after 15 January 1991 precisely because sanctions were working so well.

If the UN's prime weapon of sanctions had worked, and been seen to work, against Iraq, the standard Western argument that sanctions are ineffective (ignoring the many cases where they are used unilaterally against non-favoured nations) would lose all credibility. Sanctions could become a powerful element in the UN's arsenal against some other country which was defying its resolutions and attacking neighbouring states while sheltering behind the protection of the USA. A proven ability to enforce effective international sanctions would be an enormous boost for the UN but extremely threatening to US interests, not least in the Middle East itself. You could say that the US coalition went to war, among other reasons, to prevent the UN becoming too effective in defending the peace.

## The Superpowers and the UN

The central position of the UN, in name if not in reality, came after a long recent period when it seemed as if the superpowers were turning their backs on the organization, for different reasons.

For the Soviets it was because they have always seen it as an American tool and anyway were preoccupied at home, in Afghanistan, and in regional conflicts where they intervened directly and not through any international body.

For the Americans it was disenchantment at the UN and its agencies (UNESCO and others) for *not* observing American wishes even though, as they repeatedly argued, the USA paid most of the budget – and then the PLO got its long-desired recognition and Arafat received a hero's welcome from the General Assembly. That did it. The whole headquarters building could just float off the polluted, ugly East River into the Atlantic Ocean as far as America's foreign policy establishment was concerned.

Sadly, American attitudes to the UN are still dictated to a huge extent (although this may be diminishing) by the position the international organization takes on Israel, for the simple reason that the USA does not really have a foreign policy the way other countries do. It has domestic politics instead, with pressure groups calling the tune on foreign affairs. The Jewish lobby supports the Israeli right wing, East European exiles have kept the pure flame of anti-Communism burning, and more recently black Americans have started to exert real pressure for aid to African countries and sanctions against South Africa.

The USA has decided, for the time being at least, that it can use the UN for its own purposes – especially now that the Soviets no longer oppose it virtually automatically. It follows that it should therefore give the UN a high profile, even stoking up the old notion that the Americans are being altruistic and internationally minded in doing so. The fact is, though, that they have brought arm-twisting, blackmail and bribery of other countries to a fine art. Just because the Iraqi regime kept accusing the Americans of these tactics in mobilizing support for their position at the UN does not make that allegation false.

In the five years I spent in and around the UN in the 1970s, one of the saddest and most sobering sights was in fact the reversal of position on important issues, especially those before the Security Council, of one Third World delegation after another. They were quite open about the reason: a high-level approach by the Americans to their Foreign Minister or head of state, openly reminding them of existing aid programmes which might be withdrawn (blame Congress if need be), debt rescheduling yet to be negotiated, new packages of food aid, and economic, agricultural and above all military packages on offer – for the simple matter of a vote in their support at the UN. The USA is the market leader in this respect, although the British and French are not averse to it either. The suggestions may be more polite, perhaps more subtle, but the message is unmistakeable.

## What Exactly is the United Nations?

There is considerable confusion about this organization, with many people equating the UN with the General Assembly – which meets for a three-month session every September, with delegations from every country in the world entitled to attend (and practically all of them do). The General Assembly has no particular powers, in practice, and certainly does not have any right under the Charter to set up peacekeeping (or warmaking) operations (although the USA used the Assembly for a 'Uniting for Peace' resolution over Korea which purported to overturn the Charter on this point, when it could not get a resolution through the Security Council). The Charter carefully and specifically reserves 'peacekeeping' powers to the Security Council, a much smaller body with rotating membership, and five permanent members who were the major victorious Allies at the end of the Second World War: the USA, the Soviet Union, China, Britain and France.

The rather anomalous position of the last two is related to their history as colonial powers, and is increasingly hard to justify except possibly in terms of their officially recognized nuclear weapons capability – although both will fight to the death if necessary to keep those precious places. The fact that we and the French were the only two European powers with substantial forces in the Gulf War is no doubt related to this anomaly – as is the fact that both countries cling tenaciously to military traditions and ambitions which far outrun our economic weight, and in fact help to handicap us in the international marketplace.

The activities and role of the United Nations are generally understood in Britain in very vague terms, with strong overtones of the idealism which was so strong in regard to the UN's predecessor, the League of Nations. In particular, the Western operation in the Gulf was repeatedly described, and thereby justified, as a 'United Nations' operation.

In fact this is not a peacekeeping operation using forces under the authority of the United Nations Security Council of the sort that has been organized in the Congo, in Korea (another case where the United States wrapped itself in a UN flag – but with the distinction that it had found a way to make this officially a UN operation), in Lebanon, Cyprus, Namibia and elsewhere. Such operations have their own procedures under Article 42 of the Charter. The Security Council itself is in charge of any such action, decides how it shall be organized, and receives regular reports on it. This procedure has not been invoked in the case of the Allied attack on Iraqi forces and Iraq itself, and the countries concerned clearly had no intention of reporting back to the Security Council.

The reality of day-to-day life at United Nations headquarters in New York is that the organization acts as a mechanism, and its actions shift according to who is on the Security Council at the time, and which of the permanent members are most active and effective in using it. It therefore, naturally, takes conflicting decisions and completely fails to deal with many crucial issues of peace and war – particularly those in which any of the permanent members of the Security Council have a direct interest. The Middle East shows quite clearly that if a major power wants to block effective UN action, it can. There have been innumerable vetoes, and in the case of Israel the USA ensures that many resolutions which are passed remain ineffectual.

It is all too easy, however, to overlook the abiding strength and importance of the UN – and its specialized agencies concerned mainly with trade and economic development – even where the peacekeeping job has been blocked or distorted. For this reason alone, internationalists should support the UN and follow its operations much more than we do at present. As a diplomatic marketplace alone, the New York (and to a lesser extent the Geneva) headquarters are immensely valuable: smaller countries can conduct negotiations with each other here on issues of mutual concern, without the vast expense of permanent representation in each other's countries, or sending special delegations. Countries without diplomatic relations for political reasons (the USA and Iran, for instance) can meet discreetly in New York or in Geneva whenever they choose: nobody will notice, or care even if they do.

The UN itself has also been important in defining and focusing what is grandly called 'world opinion' on a huge range of topics. It has played a major role in defining and developing trends in Third World development and many of its issues such the role of women, the environment and the rights of children; and has been the framework within which key international treaties on outer space, the sea-bed, Antarctica and other issues are negotiated. It has also been able to make its mark on a few issues, such as decolonization worldwide and in southern Africa in particular, where the big powers refrained from blocking it.

Alignments can change; they are not set in concrete, however much it sometimes seems that way. It is certainly true that the Western powers have, before and during the Gulf War, had a field day at the UN. As the distinguished US international law expert Richard Falk has put it, there is 'the disturbing impression that the United Nations has been converted into a virtual tool of US foreign policy, thus compromising its future credibility, regardless of how the Gulf crisis turns out'. It is a situation similar to periods when the Soviet Union was boycotting the UN in protest at actions which it disagreed with – or refused to pay for – and when China was still represented not by the People's Republic but by little pro-Western Taiwan. That situation came to an end; so can the current one. In fact the American hold is remarkably fragile and could easily be upset by a shift in position of a few key players. Indeed, it seems to me that the Americans were very aware of the transient nature of the situation, which is one reason why they were so anxious to avoid any pause in the war itself, once launched, or a return to the Security Council for further discussion before its conclusion.

(It is not just the Western powers that practise manipulation, of course. The Soviets and Chinese are no mean manipulators in their own right: all's fair in love, war and international diplomacy, and I was once able to confirm that the Soviets had inserted their own wording into the Russian 'translation' of an important UN treaty. Just one of their wide repertoire of party tricks.)

The reasons for excessive US and Allied influence at the UN today are different from those that prevailed in the depths of the Cold War. They rest on the window of opportunity opened up by the Soviet Union's preoccupation with the possible break-up of the whole country as republics threaten to secede, and the accommodation with the USA over what was billed as the end of the Cold War – including, under Foreign Minister Shevardnadze, the startling decision not to oppose a US attack on Iraq. It was the Soviets, it seems, who persuaded the Chinese not to veto the key Security Council Resolution 678 which set the 15 January 1991 deadline for war.

## *Towards a New British Policy on the United Nations*
What lesson can British-based internationalists learn about how to approach this kind of crisis? What should British policy towards the United Nations be, if Labour formed the next government? What position should it, and the Liberal Democrats too, take while in opposition? How can a position be formulated which is acceptable to the mainstream Labour leadership, which could make it effective, as well as to those on the left?

My first suggestion is that we drop the references to the UN as an idealized and somehow perfect organization, a kind of international sacred cow which should be supported in all its decisions. This might be credible if UN resolutions were put together and voted on by all the nations of the world acting freely and without undue pressure from any one of the others, in accordance with both the letter and the spirit of the UN Charter. Since this is not the case, we might as well be realistic and acknowledge that we would not support all resolutions regardless. Foreign policy is a matter of national interest combined, where possible, with our interest in collective peace and security. To pretend – or even to wish – otherwise is to give up the attempt to engage in the kind of discussions which, in Britain anyway, take place far too often behind closed doors.

Especially when in opposition, we should call loudly and persist-ently for a return without delay to the UN in any international crisis, especially one where war is either threatened or actually under way. If the Labour leadership had taken this line during the war itself, it could have seriously embarrassed the government, which was claiming to be fighting the war on behalf of the UN, while being quite consistent with support for our troops. Such a position would have added weight and encouragement to the efforts of the Third World countries involved, especially Yemen, Cuba and India, to persuade the permanent members of the Security Council to stop blocking any discussion there for the duration of the war itself.

A future Labour government should give higher priority to working through the United Nations wherever possible and appro-priate, as part of a stance which cannot and will not be knee-jerk anti-American, as many on the left would like, but is part of an independent foreign policy, one which stresses co-operation at international level – with any country of goodwill. In order to achieve a serious change in this direction it will be necessary to appoint a political nominee (supported, ideally, by one or more sympathetic advisers) as Permanent Representative to the UN. The previous Labour government did this with the appointment of Ivor Richards in the late 1960s, even making him a member of the Cabinet. This obviously did not mean anything in reality, since it is difficult to attend Cabinet meetings in Downing Street when you are in New York. The principle which counts is real backing (and being seen to be backed) by your government at the highest level; regular consultations and involvement in the policy deliberations, not just presentation; and a mandate to take initiatives.

Labour in particular seems to have great difficulty assessing the importance of Britain at an international level. I attended one policy discussion about the UN where speaker after speaker stressed the unimportance – indeed, the irrelevance – of Britain in the context of world affairs. Since we are so insignificant, it therefore follows that our best policy is a sort of sub-Scandinavian: all ideals but little influence.

This is complete rubbish. Britain is a very important player on the international scene, and extremely influential at international gatherings. Not only is it still one of the largest economies in the world, it also has a unique position for largely historical reasons – as a permanent member of the Security Council, as an important member of the European Group and especially of the EC and – despite those who consider this something of a joke – because of its very close and friendly relations with other English-speaking countries, which means mainly the Commonwealth. Such matters as training many of their diplomats and allied services to follow our ways of thinking and operating are extremely important (as the Americans have discovered, but much more recently).

The Scandinavian position on the UN, which is often cited as the model for what British policy on it should be, is not necessarily the whole answer. The policies of Scandinavian countries are not always as full of sweetness and light as some like to imagine, in any case – especially those of Sweden. There are important elements that we can adopt, but Britain is different because we have much more weight – and, whether we like it or not, many more economic interests at stake.

Many decisions at international conferences are arrived at by regional blocs meeting separately to formulate their positions, followed by negotiations between their representatives to arrive at the final resolution, which is then formally voted on. Britain can swing whole voting blocs in international forums in many situations, if it shifts its own policy significantly (and even more strongly if we act in co-operation with the French.) This applies not just to issues of war and peace, but to virtually the whole range of international negotiation within the general UN framework which is so crucial to much of modern life. As a trading nation, as well as a military one, Britain has a particular role to play in issues of international economics as well as the more dramatic arena of pure diplomacy.

The task for a new Labour government is to start using the influence we have in the direction of a more independent policy, and a much less warlike one. The obvious starting points are a shift away from automatic support for the USA; a much closer alignment with the French, at least on some issues; and closer consultations with leading Third World countries which themselves play a key role in regional as well as international organizations, such as Nigeria and India.

And the United Nations itself? If a future British government wanted to support the UN and its agencies as a matter of principle, the grim choice may first have to be partially to destroy it. I have in mind the virtual stranglehold which the United States has acquired on the UN budget: the financial demands of the organization itself are huge, and the USA not only provides most of the money but has adopted the old Soviet tactic of paying in arrears, so keeping the organization in a state of constant desperation to retain American goodwill.

It is a lesson the Americans learnt when they brought UNESCO to heel, and they will lose this control only if the UN learns to prune its budget drastically, rids itself of the vast number of expensive time-servers and time-wasters it currently employs, and takes drastic action against the corruption of the Secretariat which makes it a hotbed of nepotism, tribalism, racism, sexism and factionalism of every conceivable kind. (In 1975, International Women's Year, I was involved in a small group in the UN Secretariat which conducted a survey on discrimination. The results were horrific; the Secretariat's reaction was repressive, to say the least. My own conclusion was that in examining one area of favouritism and discrimination, we had uncovered an entire system. My sources tell me that if anything, the situation has got even worse since then.)

One aspect of a clean-up of the UN Secretariat and of the worse UN agencies (the Food and Agriculture Organization and World Food Programme being prime candidates) should be a British lead in orchestrating a return by member states to a stance of non-intervention in Secretariat appointments: in other words, no more telling the Secretary-General to appoint British nominees to senior posts in order to look after British interests. Britain was, to our credit, one of the last countries to start doing this; we should now lead the way back to respect for a genuinely international civil service. Otherwise all the resolutions in the world will not achieve a satisfactory job for the United Nations.

I do not suggest for one moment that the clean-up would be an easy job – but it has to be done. The UN could probably operate on half its current budget if it employed the best candidate for the job (subject to national quotas) and got its money's worth of work from him or her. An essential step would be the appointment of a Secretary-General with the specific brief of doing this, rather than one who is virtually guaranteed to do nothing to disturb the status quo unless under specific instructions from the major powers.

## Conclusion

The cliff-hanging story of the UN Security Council's involvement and exclusion from the war in the Gulf is a sobering one. World opinion against the war, and the way the Americans pursued it, was not permitted a voice in the UN. In Britain, as in other Western countries, there was undoubted confusion and unhappiness among the majority of people, who were offered no alternative to support-ing 'our boys' – not even a partial alternative offered in the form of an Opposition call to return to the UN. (Calls for an immediate conference on the whole future of the Middle East were not nearly so realistic.) Instead, we had Labour, Liberal Democrat and Green calls to 'support the UN' as synonymous with supporting the war.

If this kind of crisis ever happens again, we must be prepared to take a more realistic line: not the UN right or wrong, but support for initiatives that match up with the purposes of the original Charter. Looking further beyond this, a future Labour government needs to work with and through the UN and its agencies in a way which is consistent with our best interests, while offering a substantial shift in favour of effective international co-operation both to keep the peace and to preserve and improve life on this fragile planet of ours.

# ROGER OWEN

## Epilogue
## Making Sense of an Earthquake:
## The Middle East after the Gulf War

Sitting in the gardens of the Marriott Hotel in Cairo a month after the end of the Gulf War, I saw a young woman wearing a T-shirt with the words 'Kuwait is Free thanks to Mr Bush' on the front and 'See you in Free Kuwait' on the back. Perhaps, for her, things really were that simple.

But we also know that wars bring changes, that the one thing the use of force can never do is to turn back the clock.

What are these changes? How were they generated? And what effect will they have on the Middle East over the next few years? Finding answers to the questions may help us approach the more basic conundrum of what did the war mean.

As a historian I can only try to begin at the beginning. I know, of course, that disputes about the causes of some conflicts – for example the First World War – generate a huge literature and are unlikely ever to be brought to a satisfactory conclusion. However, in this case, the origins of the Iraqi invasion of Kuwait do seem to be traceable directly to the end of the eight year Iran/Iraq war which left Iraq with a huge army and huge debts. Why Saddam Hussein should then have decided not to disarm but to pursue a policy of trying to provide his country with more guns as well as more butter is difficult to explain. But it seems reasonable to argue that it was the financial strain which this involved, as well as his inability to re-establish satisfactory control over the leadership of his peace-time army, which drove him on to find compensation in Kuwait.

Historians seeking to answer the question of whether he could either have been stopped or diverted at this stage will inevitably begin their analysis by looking at the weeks just before and just after the invasion of 2 August. Could the United States have given Saddam Hussein a warning blunt enough to stop him in his tracks? And, in the days immediately after the invasion, is King Husain correct in asserting that the occupation was a bargaining counter and that Saddam Hussein would have withdrawn his troops almost at once if the Egyptians and Saudis had not forced the majority of the Arab states to condemn him out of hand?

After that, it looks very much as though Presidents Bush and Hussein locked themselves on a collision course which no third party mediator could have hoped to halt. On the one hand, Bush was determined that Saddam Hussein should abandon Kuwait without compensation. On the other, Saddam was almost certainly expressing a deeply held conviction when he told Tony Benn and other visitors that withdrawal would mean the collapse of Iraqi civilian and, most importantly, military morale. There is some evidence that he may also have comforted himself and his close colleagues with his belief that, by filling Kuwait with more and more troops and surrounding it with more and more defensive structures, he could make sure that the United States would never dare to attack.

If this is correct, both leaders had too much at stake to be able to back down. For Bush, the crisis was a very personal test of his leadership not only of the United States but also of the putative American-dominated international alliance which he hoped to use to maintain world order in the post-Cold War era. For Saddam Hussein, it was also a test of a type of leadership based on willpower, toughness and, above all, on the need to prove – to his colleagues as much as to his people – that he was always correct in his calculations, that he was incapable of mistakes. Calling him a 'butcher' is in some ways a complement to his ruthlessness; but to accuse him of 'miscalculation' – as James Baker did at his Geneva talks with Tariq Aziq just before the war – was about the worst insult anyone could make.

Does this then mean that all attempts at mediation were doomed in advance or that sanctions could not possibly have worked? As far as the former is concerned, we must await the testimony of the Russian envoy, Mr Primakov, the one mediator who seems to have been trusted by both sides. From his comments so far he would seem to have been generally pessimistic about his chances except just before the war broke out when he appeared to think that, if Saddam Hussein had agreed to withdraw his troops at the very last minute, he might have avoided disaster. As it happened, Saddam Hussein responded too slowly, for reasons which had everything to do with his own character and his own underestimate of the dangers he faced. But, even if he had acted with greater speed, it is unlikely that the Americans and their partners would have allowed him to get away with anything but the most humiliating of surrenders.

As for arguments about the efficacy of sanctions, these work both ways. Given Saddam Hussein's determination to stay put, it is unlikely that economic pressure would have worked in the short or medium term. However, by the same token, the experience of severe domestic hardship inside Iraq itself was probably the only thing which would have persuaded him to leave peacefully in the longer run.

Meanwhile, it took people in the rest of the world some time even to begin to understand the true nature of what was going on. As far as many in the West were concerned, the three or four months necessary for the Allied troops to get into position along the Kuwaiti and Iraqi border was a golden opportunity either to explore the possibility of mediation or to take part in a debate about the pros and cons of the use of force. Articles were written, conferences and workshops held, friendships strained to near breaking point, but all with singularly little effect on the actual conduct or policy.

Looked at from the point of view of those who wanted to stop the war, we can see how their arguments suffered from certain deep-rooted flaws. They were based on the assumption that they were dealing with rational men pursuing comprehensible national

**161**

interests and systematically ruled out the possibility that what seemed like common sense in London or Washington looked quite different when judged in terms of the necessities of staying in power in Baghdad.

There was also the inevitable temptation to try to drive home the argument by exaggerating the possible consequences of a prolonged conflict. This was a particular problem for people like myself whose thinking was very much guided by the fear that recourse to war in the Middle East would only make things worse than they already were. The mantle of a Cassandra is never much fun at the best of times. However, if you do want to use it to influence policy you have to be in a position to make reasonable predictions about a complex situation with a large number of possible outcomes. It is one thing to observe, as many did in 1956 or 1957, that a Middle Eastern war has acted like an earthquake; quite another to anticipate correctly where the cracks will appear or which structures have been most fatally undermined. In retrospect, we can see that those who predicted an oil price of $80 a barrel, or the use of American tactical nuclear weapons, or the immediate overthrow of the Egyptian government by an enraged population, singularly failed to convince. Were those who might have predicted a Kurdish uprising, followed by a mass exodus of several million people, listened to with any greater attention?

Beyond this, however, there were tougher barriers to getting an anti-war message across, at least as far as Britain was concerned. The troops were already on their way. The Labour and Liberal parties, both of which had taken the lead in opposing the Suez expedition in 1956, now firmly supported government policy, and, perhaps most important of all, the weight of recent historical experience encouraged popular support for a war to be fought shoulder to shoulder with our old American ally by a professional army deployed at some distance from our shores. Elsewhere in Europe it was different of course; recent German historical experience pointed in quite the opposite direction. Nevertheless, there too, polls showed that a majority believed in the use of force against

Iraq even before news of the emotionally charged Scud missile attacks on Israel.

As for the Middle East itself, while elites carefully weighed up the advantages and disadvantages of supporting one side or the other, the peoples of the Eastern end of the Arab world appeared to be engaged in quite a different type of discourse reflecting a whole gamut of emotions from triumphalism to fear. When it reached outside ears it was likely to stress the importance of Saddam Hussein's exposure of a long history of Western hypocrisy or double standards – most notably over Palestine. But when shared with friends, its more obvious feature was the tension between a desire to believe in his ability to mount a serious challenge to American and Israeli interests and an obvious effort not to allow all powers of judgement to be swept aside. 'He was playing with our emotions', as one Egyptian friend later put it. Meanwhile, in North Africa, there was an often lively public debate between supporters and opponents of the war, leading to deep-rooted splits inside most religious organizations and oppositional political parties.

Few people will forget the war itself or, rather, what we were allowed to learn of it via the babble of talk and the carefully contrived photos. The speed of the final victory in Kuwait defied the predictions of all but the most enthusiastic apostles of high-tech bombing campaigns. But few could have imagined that Saddam Hussein would make things so much more worse for his troops by ordering their chaotic withdrawal on the second day of the land offensive, even if we can now see that he needed his elite forces for the inevitable second stage against the Kurdish and Shiite rebellions in the north and south.

Then came the consequences. According to the Coalition's plan, backed by the Security Council of the United Nations, the war was supposed to lead to the freeing of Kuwait and the return of the Kuwaiti ruling family, but not to the dismemberment of Iraq nor, it would now seem, the forcible overthrow of Saddam Hussein by Allied troops. In other words, in spite of the challenge which

Saddam Hussein had posed to the whole post-colonial order in the Middle East – to the legitimacy of borders and regimes, to the distribution of wealth between those with oil and those without, to the dispossession of the Palestinians, to the special relations which still existed between the United States and its Arab allies – the lid was to be put back on again and, with only a few concessions to Arab public opinion, kept tightly shut. However, as we know, no sooner was the fighting over in Kuwait than major cracks in the old order began to appear.

Not surprisingly, the first stresses and strains appeared inside Iraq and Kuwait themselves. As far as Iraq was concerned, the loss of authority in Baghdad and the disruption of mechanisms of government control outside the capital due to Allied bombing encouraged a challenge from Kurdish and Shiite groups so immediate and spontaneous that it would probably have taken place even without American encouragement. The result was the temporary seizure of many of the larger towns from which the majority of their inhabitants then fled in panic as the tide of battle quickly turned and the Allies refused all pleas to intervene. The consequences in terms of suffering and destruction are almost impossible to comprehend. The test is now whether Saddam Hussein's regime, based on a combination of fear and promise of material reward, can survive in the new world of sanctions, reparations, reduced income and carefully-contrived international humiliation.

The political future of Kuwait seems equally uncertain. Apart from the social tensions and unruly passions aroused by the Iraqi invasion, there is a major question mark against the leadership of the Al-Sabah family itself and its ability both to re-establish its authority and then to find some way of meeting demands for greater accountability and popular participation in government. Like other ruling families, the Al-Sabahs used the breathing space provided by British protection before 1961 to develop some of the skills needed to run a modern administration and oil economy. But during the 1980s they encountered a series of increasingly dangerous challenges, from the Iran/Iraq War through the crash of the unofficial stock exchange in 1982 to the Iraqi campaign of threats just before the occupation in 1990, which stretched them to the limits. Now the Al-Sabahs face their greatest challenge of all, which is to lead their deeply divided community through a prolonged period of political, economic and social reconstruction including, according to present plans, a huge reduction in the resident foreign community on which, until now, the Kuwaits have relied for almost all their public and personal services. On top of this, they also know that their previous experiences of trying to share government with an elected National Assembly have not been happy ones. On two occasions, in 1976 and again in 1986, the Assembly was dissolved largely because some of its members had been too vocal in their criticisms of cabinet ministers who were also leading members of the Al-Sabah family. And there is now every likelihood that this same situation will recur once the assembly is revived yet again as promised.

What happens in Iraq and Kuwait will be closely watched by neighbouring regimes which share many of the same characteristics and face many of the same challenges in the post-Gulf War era. Behind Iraq stands Syria with a similar system of political control that will prove almost as difficult for its architect – President Hafez al-Asad – to alter without throwing all his power away. And behind Kuwait stand all the other family states, including Saudi Arabia, whose rulers have also signally failed to look after their own system of national defence and so remain equally open to the criticism that they have been forced to rely on outside, and predominantly American, military support. They too depend on a type of rule in which all the major cabinet offices are controlled by members of the ruling family. They too know how difficult it would be to share power with any elected council or assembly whose criticisms, however constructive, would inevitably be taken as a challenge to their own authority. As for the bottom line: if the ruling families don't take personal charge of defence and internal security or economic management, what are they there for at all? In these circumstances little progress towards political participation can be expected while the rulers will be even more firmly convinced that they must stand together or face the consequences. It is even possible to imagine a situation in which, should the Al-Sabahs run into serious domestic difficulty, the result might be a second occupation of Kuwait, but this time by the forces of the other Gulf states determined to arrest any further threat to royal authority.

Outside the Gulf the war produced a series of more mixed effects. As far as governments were concerned, those that supported the Coalition – like Egypt and Syria – were well placed to enjoy an immediate financial reward. In the case of Egypt this in turn emboldened its rulers to sign an agreement with the international Monetary Fund and the World Bank, designed, in part, to take advantage of these favourable circumstances to encourage a huge reduction in its debt by its major creditors grouped together in the so-called 'Club of Paris'. It also used some of its windfall profits to establish various social funds which it hoped would cushion the shock of the substantial price rises demanded by the IMF as part of the same agreement. Whether this would work to prevent serious unrest was another matter. While the government benefited financially from the war, the people, as a rule, suffered a considerable loss of income as a result of the reduced remittances of Egyptian workers employed in the Gulf. Now they faced even further hardships from higher energy prices and a new Value Added Tax levied on most articles of mass consumption.

As for the opposition movements, where they existed in the Arab world they usually suffered a damaging split between those who supported the war and those who were against. This was particularly apparent in the case of those religious movements like the Muslim Brothers in Egypt, the Nahda in Tunisia and the FIS (Islamic Salvation Front) in Algeria which relied heavily on Saudi Arabia for funds and support. Some members felt that they had to go along with Saudi policy however unsatisfactory; others believed that the main enemy was the United States and that any further expansion of American influence had to be resisted at all costs. The fact that the Iranian revolutionaries, to whom some still looked for guidance, remained neutral as between Iraq and the United States only made matters more difficult. Leftist groups such as the Egyptian Progressives were also split between those who believed that the Iraqi occupation of Kuwait should be ended by force and those who advocated either an Arab solution to the problem or direct support for Iraq against American attack. Such divisions deprived the anti-war movement in the Arab world of vital leadership at a time when it might have been possible to get large crowds out on the streets once the ground war began in February 1991. This was particularly the case in Egypt where heavy policing managed to prevent demonstrations of no more than a few thousand people at most.

The result was a severe check to any hopes of either a united Arab or a united religious response to the war. Indeed, there are many who make the point that the forces of Islamic renewal received a major blow to their claims to represent a homogeneous, region-wide movement. But this is too simple a claim. While Arab governments and elites were certainly divided between those who supported the war and those who opposed it, there is every indication that the vast majority of the Arab peoples outside the Arabian peninsula opposed the American-led coalition. And it follows that, even if Arab unity is still a dream, popular feelings of Arabism and Arab solidarity are as alive as they ever were – perhaps even more so if the huge size of the demonstrations in Morocco, right at the opposite end of the Arab world to Iraq and Kuwait, are to be taken as a guide. However, as always, such sentiments require guidance and leadership if they are to make a coherent impact across present state boundaries. The same is probably just as true of the religious feelings represented in the larger Islamic groups which, at the moment, are organized primarily to compete for power within national political arenas.

Apart from the Kurds, those who suffered most immediately from the war were that other stateless Middle Eastern people, the Palestinians. Confined to their houses as a result of prolonged curfews in the West Bank and Gaza, losing their jobs in the Gulf states or enduring both Iraqi occupation and then the perils of liberation in Kuwait itself, they lost resources, political advantage and, perhaps most important of all, hope. Few believed that victory for an American-ised Coalition would be to their benefit and it is not difficult to see why. The comprehensive defeat of Iraq deprived the Arab world of the one military force which appeared able to pose any sort of challenge to the Israelis. Meanwhile, the Israeli government itself was able to manage the opportunities provided by the war with sufficient skill to rebuild its damaged relationship with the United States. In these circumstances, a combination of despair and frustration drove even the most level-headed of the elite to support the Iraqi position with an enthusiasm which puzzled outsiders but which was perfectly comprehensible to those who observed it – and, more importantly, felt it – at close quarters.

It was this same deep sense of bitterness and betrayal which led Yasser Arafat to abandon one of the two most important bedrocks of his political position and to identify the PLO so closely with the interests of a single Arab regime. That he did so can only be explained in terms of his other basic necessity; the need to maintain Palestinian national unity at a time when the tide of pro-Iraqi feelings was running so strong. Nevertheless, the price he paid was a heavy one. He lost financial support from the Gulf states, he gave the Americans the excuse they needed to ignore him and, altogether, he ensured that the PLO was relegated to a marginal diplomatic position from which it will take a long time to recover. Nevertheless, provided he can overcome any attempt by a major Arab regime either to replace him or to create a rival organization, his leadership will certainly survive. But to do this he will depend more on more on being able to maintain the overwhelming support of the Palestinians in the West Bank and Gaza who are now far and away his most important political constituency.

As for the Middle East's three major non-Arab states, Iran, Israel and Turkey, each one was able to derive considerable short-term advantage from the war itself. All benefited from the destruction of Saddam Hussein's war-making potential; all seized the opportunity to improve their relations with the United States and its Coalition partners. Nevertheless, in the slightly longer-run, various problems also presented themselves which would require very careful handling. For Turkey, this was the question of the Kurds and of how to prevent pressures for Kurdish autonomy in Iraq from encouraging similar demands from among their own Kurdish population. For Israel, it was the certainty that the United States would use its victory to make at least one more effort to settle the Palestinian issue. And for the Iranian leadership, it was not only the problems of more than a million Kurdish refugees but also of how to obtain Western recognition and Western investment while still rejecting a permanent American influence in the Gulf region. I will return to these points when I come to consider the question of peace and a new Middle Eastern order.

We in the West are taught to believe that wars should teach lessons – although a better way of putting it would be that they serve to remind us of things we already know. We are also taught that they should end in a peace conference designed to prevent similar wars from breaking out in future and, if possible, to make the world a generally better place in which to live. How does the Gulf War fit into this perspective?

As far as the lessons – or reminders – are concerned, two stand out. The first is that the United Nations was originally established after the Second World War as a club for the victors in the war against Germany and Japan with a mechanism – the Security Council with its five permanent members – designed to allow the Great Powers to serve as the architects and then supervisors of the new international order. This may be small comfort to those in the Middle East who complain that the United States has used the Gulf crisis to hijack the organization for its own ends. But it does remind us that it was only because of the Cold War and the Chinese revolution that the Security Council lost much of its original power, creating a vacuum which the Secretary General and the General Assembly – with its greatly expanded membership of former colonial states – could only partially fill. Now, as a result of

Mr Gorbachev's new policies and Russian and Chinese economic weakness, we are back roughly to the situation as it was in 1946 with the Great Powers firmly in the saddle again and possessed of enormous influence over issues about which they can all agree.

What the states of the Middle East can do about this new situation is another matter and will take some time to work out. They can try to ally themselves with the United States and rely on its veto for protection. They can wait and hope that new, and stronger, regimes will emerge in the USSR and China more willing to stand up to American domination. Or more constructively, they can try to reform the United Nation's practice in such a way as to restore some of its hard-won international character without which it is in danger or becoming simply the instrument of its Great Power founders.

The second lesson concerns the way in which democracies conduct their foreign policies and, more especially, go to war. This has been well-documented as far as the United States is concerned. But it still comes as something of a shock to hear that particular mixture of morality, chauvinism and undiluted self-interest which an American President must use to encourage his people forward into battle. It is at this moment that the foreign policy of a democracy can be seen most clearly for what it is: part and parcel of domestic policy with similar expectations concerning its justice, its expediency and its value for money. Certain kinds of appeal are absolutely necessary if the electorate is going to be persuaded to give up its treasure and to countenance the spilling of its blood. One technique is, of course, to demonize the enemy – for why else should such a huge effort be made to bring him down? Another is to underline the assumptions, already referred to, that wars ought to teach lessons and to end in a greater good for all. By the same token, opponents of such wars are driven to try to undercut or de-legitimise support for them by arguing that they are undertaken primarily for base motives such as the search for profit or cheap oil.

However, while the observation that democracies need to prepare themselves for war in a certain kind of way is helpful in explaining aspects of Western policy, it misses one of the major peculiarities of the Gulf War which is that, as far as the American and European members of the Coalition were concerned, it cost very little blood and may even have turned an accountant's profit due to Saudi and other subventions. Furthermore, thanks again to the Saudis and their ability to increase oil output, there was only the tiniest rise in the price of petrol. And this in turn raises the question of whether the search for lessons need be quite as energetic if so much has been gained at so little cost? My answer to this is that, although the need to make political sense of a war is lessened in such circumstances, it does not really matter. If, of necessity, it takes a great deal of effort to cajole democracies into a major war, then each new case has to be argued on its own merits. Moreover, although lessons from previous crises may be available for rhetorical purposes – for example, the need to stand up to a Hitler, to avoid another Vietnam – they do not provide any kind of precedent binding on future political leaders.

I am tempted to mention a third lesson involving some of the consequences of what was the world's first war by television. However, the experience is still too raw to be able to analyse it with any kind of objectivity and I will content myself simply with one comment. This is that television required such an instant and continuous outpouring of words that it was virtually impossible for the presenters and experts to step outside their own preconceived ways of thought, to reflect quietly about what was going on or to listen to other types of discourse – particularly what was being said among Middle Easterners themselves. The result was another contribution to the phenomenon of 'deafness' mentioned by John Berger: the deafness of those who spend so much time talking and pontificating that they have no time to hear anyone but themselves.

Given their much closer involvement in the crisis, the lessons drawn by the Arabs were bound to be more various and to take longer to elaborate. Nevertheless, there was soon a lively debate which in its Cairo form began to move towards the following consensus. First, Arab regimes and Arab boundaries remained sacrosanct and no effort should be made to try to alter them by force. Second, Saddam Hussein's appeal to the Arab peoples had been powerful – and dangerous – enough to require a measured response. This should start by addressing his demand for a better distribution of wealth between the oil-rich and the oil-poor states as well as the vexed question of Palestine. The latter would be best achieved by an international conference at which all the interested parties were represented. Third, a reformed Arab League under Egyptian guidance should work out an improved framework for intra-Arab cooperation and for settling intra-Arab disputes. Fourth, arrangements for the future security of the Gulf should be arranged by the Gulf states themselves in cooperation with Syria and Egypt, but with only limited support from the United States. Fifth, what became known after the Damascus Declaration of March 1991 as the Six Plus Two arrangement (that is the Gulf states plus Egypt and Syria) might be expanded to encompass other interested parties, most notably the Iranians with whom Egypt was quick to re-establish diplomatic relations.

Elsewhere in the Arab world the discussion took a different turn. In the Gulf, behind closed doors, the major lesson of the war was that self-defence was still impossible, that larger armies would absorb much-needed manpower while increasing the possibility of a military coup and that, in these circumstances there was nothing for it but continued reliance on support from American troops either quartered in local bases or ready to re-occupy Saudi and other airfields and barracks at a moment's notice. The major problem then was how to convey this unpalatable truth to restive local populations. In countries like Syria and Jordan, on the other hand, discussions inevitably stressed the importance of Arab unity while seeking to interpret the significance of the challenge posed by Saddam Hussein and the nature of his appeal to so large a spectrum of Arab thought.

The assumption that the making of a war should be followed by the making of a peace played an equally powerful role in the Gulf crisis. It was the belief that to join the coalition would be to assure one's country of a seat at the conference and a voice in the making of the new world order, which President Bush was so quick to proclaim, that led many regimes like the Turks to sign up with the United States and Britain in the first place. Once again, memories of what had happened at the end of the second World War loomed large.

In the event, however, the United States was left to make most of the running itself. For one thing, the President and his Secretary of State had laid out their set of four guiding principles very early in the crisis. These were attention to Gulf Security, arms control, a solution to the Arab/Israeli/Palestinian conflict and the establish-ment of some mechanism for Middle Eastern economic develop-ment. For another, the Europeans were unable either to come up with a unified policy of their own or, like Britain, to do more than try to elaborate on some of these same principles themselves. Just as important, the Americans had, consciously or unconsciously, revealed yet another of the Gulf War's significant peculiarities when they had decided to combine an imposed cease-fire with Iraq with a conference to settle the wider problems of the Middle East all in one go. Historical precedent would seem to have demanded a negotiated settlement between Iraq and its neighbours supported by their Coalition allies. But in this case, President Bush, having eschewed any talk of linkage in the run up to the war, was now apparently ready to echo Saddam Hussein's assertion that all Middle Eastern problems were inter-connected and need to be solved in one general package.

Just how this is to be done remains to be seen. In the weeks that followed the ending of the war, several of America's principles seemed to be watered down and the notion that they were all inter-related ignored. While Gulf security was supposed to have been taken care of by the promise of both Egyptian/Syrian and United States military assistance, plans for regional economic development were downgraded in response to the discovery that its most likely pay-masters, Saudi Arabia and Kuwait, had earmarked most of their own resources and were probably going to have to borrow from the international financial community themselves. As for arms control, this was now deemed to apply only to so-called weapons of mass destruction – defined as chemical, biological and nuclear – and then just to Iraq, until that utopian moment when the United States plucked up its courage to tackle the issue of Israeli stocks of these same deadly ingredients.

This left the Arab/Israeli/Palaestinian issue which the Americans tried to address with their famous 'two-track' approach involving simultaneous confidence-building measures between Israel and its Arab neighbours and Israel and the Palestinians. Given the fact that the Israeli cabinet contained so many hardliners, that the Likud Block gained popular support during the war and that its leader and Prime Minister, Mr Shamir, was a master at doing nothing at all, the United States faced a formidable task. Nevertheless, the fact that Israel had not used the war to try to expel large numbers of Palestinians provided a small indication of what might lie ahead. For the Israeli do-nothings, the experience of the wartime curfews in the West Bank proved that the Intifada (the Palestinian uprising) could be contained indefinitely without too much trouble. But for others in the Likud and the Labour Alignment, the continued presence of a large Palestinian population without citizenship or their own passports was an anomaly which must one day be addressed. From this perception came talk of internal autonomy as well as, more speculatively, the possibility of a species of arrangement by which the inhabitants of the West Bank and Gaza would be offered Jordanian or some other kind of Arab nationality. Whether or not they, or the Jordanians or the PLO, could be brought to agree to such a plan was quite another matter.

From a Middle Eastern, and particularly from an Arab, perspective this is all very puzzling. Not surprisingly, those on the receiving end of what they call the new American 'order' want to know what it will look like before they make up their mind whether to try to find a place in it for themselves or to resist it as best they can. As it is, they are left with the impression of a significant build up of US power without much idea as to how it is to be exercised in a regular way. They believe firmly, for example, that oil prices will remain low as a result of the American alliance with Saudi Arabia which makes it, in effect, an honorary member of OPEC. They see two non-Arab states, Israel and Turkey, as Washington's major military partners in the region. They expect more direct interventions in their own affairs. For the rest, they wait – expectantly or fearfully as the case may be – for President Bush to reveal his hand.

One last question concerns the way in which the war and its consequences may look in the longer run. As the states of the Middle East try to cope with the new world of Western dominance and Eastern perestroika, as they prepare for the huge challenges of the 21st century, how much difference will the war be seen to have made? Will it, as many fear, help to confirm the Middle East's status as an international backwater defined by its distinctly un-modern obsessions with religion, intolerance and one man or family rule? Or will it appear as simply a tiny diversion on the way towards a more democratic, more peaceful, future?

The answer depends on where you look. As far as the Arab states of North Africa are concerned, the one country which lost heavily from the war was Sudan whose regime discouraged inter-national support more than ever by its identification with Saddam Hussein, leaving it weaker and even less well able to cope with the huge internal problems of famine and civil strife. In Egypt, Tunisia, Algeria and Morocco, however, the agenda, set well before the Gulf crisis, of economic reconstruction accompanied by tentative political liberalization will be seen to have continued, and perhaps even accelerated, as a result of the war. In Egypt, it provided a filip to further reform, as already described. Elsewhere, the divisions created within the opposition – both religious and leftist – will allow regimes to be somewhat more bold in their tolerance of political diversity provided, of course, that their economies respond to the harsh measures prescribed by the IMF and World Bank.

And all the time there will pressure from the Economic Community, just across the Mediterranean, for further reform.

At the eastern end of the Arab World it is quite another story. There, the particular mix of hot spots, unsolved problems and potential flash points will probably be seen to have been made much more dangerously explosive – at least in the short run. The West Bank and Gaza, Lebanon, the political future of the authoritarian regimes in Syria and Iraq, the continued existence of Jordan, the future of family rule not just in Kuwait but all over the Arabian peninsula, the relations between the Arabs and the non-Arab powers like Iran, Israel and Turkey: none of these issues have been made any better by the war – with the possible exception of Lebanon – and many rendered more complicated and unmanagable. Other dangers lurk as well. As the Iraqi occupation of Kuwait has proved, oil wells are more vulnerable to sabotage than anyone had previously imagined. America's new energy policy, developed while the war itself was in progress, foresees a continued dependence on cheap oil imports which, in turn, implies the possibility of further interventions in the Gulf should security or supply be endangered. The states of the Arabian peninsula continue to pursue contradictory policies towards their migrant workforces, unable to prevent their citizens from importing unlimited supplies of cheap labour at some times, trying to restrict it on political grounds the next, and all the time treating their migrant populations with such a flagrant disregard for their human rights as to store up a great deal of trouble for the future.

In such difficult circumstances, any hopes that all these conflicts can be solved in one gigantic peace conference are bound to be disappointed. But it would be equally foolish to imagine that the pre-war status quo can be painlessly re-established, even without the malevolent presence of Saddam Hussein. Cracks in social structures will widen, political systems will sway or tumble, just as they did after the Anglo-French and Israeli attack on Suez in 1956 which led, over time, to the overthrow of the Iraqi monarchy, the brief union between Egypt and Syria and, some would argue, the outbreak of the 1967 Middle Eastern war. This is not an environment that encourages new initiatives by those on the inside: Gulf rulers will use the new security system not to protect themselves from outside attack but from domestic opposition; President Asad, just like Prime Minister Itzhak Shamir, will be remembered more for his obduracy and his ability to withstand outside pressure than for his willingness to meet problems with programmes of constructive reform. But change will certainly come as the frustrations exposed by Saddam Hussein intensify. And, the eastern end of the Arab world being what it is, some of them will be violent and very destructive.

If any one person is to be held responsible for setting all this in train it is, of course, Saddam Hussein himself. Just how he managed to get into a position of such power is still a matter of dispute. To some he is simply a ruthless thug who was lucky enough to be able to take over an oil-rich state at a time when there were all the revenues he could possibly need to establish the army, the security apparatuses and the public services on which his system of control depends. Others stress his organizational skills, his admiration for Stalin and Lenin, and the fact that he managed to turn the small and divided Iraqi Ba'ath party into an instrument which reached down through Iraqi society to control most parts of the country on a street by street, village by village, basis. In fact both perspectives are an essential part of the explanation. Together they nourished not only the cult of the personality which developed as soon as he assumed full powers as President in 1979, but also Saddam Hussein's own aspirations towards a totalitarian control over every aspect of Iraqi life and thought. However, this could not be. A wartime army of a million men cannot be controlled by the same methods used to cow a fearful citizenry. Torture and terror could not be routinised as they were under most Communist regimes in Eastern Europe but remained an ever-present reality, dissolving old ties and allegiances and allowing nothing to take their place except a kind of fearful and uneasy sectarianism. This was the unstable mix which encouraged war, aggression and then, whenever Saddam Hussein's control was relaxed, mutiny and rebellion.

In the months before the fighting began I watched Saddam Hussein as much as possible on television. However weary his eyes, his face seemed taughter than before, the adrenalin seemed to be flowing, it was as though he enjoyed riding this particular dangerous wave. Then came the crash. We are now waiting to see if he has the willpower, the determination, necessary to re-establish his fearful system yet again. He certainly has neither the wisdom nor the capacity for compromise and persuasion to do anything else.

# AUTOBIOGRAPHY

*Sadiq al Saygh*

In the twentieth century
On the left corner of the Third World
Between two rivers and a closed cloud
A poet, lonely poet, was born, asking:
Did I come to the right place
At the right time?
Will it be generous and forgiving to me?
Will my face be acceptable to it?
Am I going to be accountable for my skin's colour?
For my origin of race?
Is there a house for a person like me?
Will I be given enough bread?
Enough warmth?
Enough love?
Or am I to be killed,
To be charged for my way of thinking?
Am I going to be sent to unknown wars?
In unknown countries?
At the end the poet asks:
What is to be done?
Am I to be the bird or the bullet?
The injured heart or the spear?
The sword or the severed head?

In the left part of the Third World
In a certain corner

Close to a white cloud
A poet was born.
His midwife lulled him in her arms
And said:
'A nice face
But vague –
I do not like his way of looking.'
One of his relatives said:
'A crazy light is in his eyes.'
His teacher said:
'My God!
He seems like Jesus
And disobedience at one and the same time.'
His mother said:
'I hear a strange tortured voice inside him.'

Between a junction of two centuries
Adjacent to a police station
And muddy old house
Among hungry dogs
And midnight litter
Near a river traveling to unknown places
The poet grew up.
His voice began to be free as the wind,
His poetry-reading like the rustle of leaves.
He liked to sleep under the date palms
Following the moving clouds.
He also liked the sea
Interrogation of the waves
Deep in censored books
Running on the horse of the age
To his unknown destiny.
In his eyes was a deep hunger for the truth and justice,
His parts were mixed with the sun,
Unaware of what was burning inside him

Nor knowing what he was –
A bird or a bullet
A heart or a dagger
A sword or a severed head.


The poet grew up.
He read the holy Koran, the Bible, the Old Testament
    and *Das Kapital*.
His entrepreneur – each of us has his own entrepreneur –
Told him:
'Since the beginning of time
There is a seller and one who is for sale.
Since the beginning of the world
The human beings were the commodities
And man is liable to be sold,
Brought up by his anger,
By others' violence,
Preserved by his delicate balance.'
He knew that poets are divided into two groups:
The first searching for his food like a dog,
The second has nothing but his vision
His fever
His agonies
Day after day. He noticed
That even his face began to change.
Unlike other poets'
His face became sweeter.
His tortured eyes, although full of uncertain death,
Could look through the most difficult avenues.
His heart began to think,
Refusing his old way of intuition
From the other side.
He neglected what he had been taught about
    the purposes of poetry.
He even purposely ignored the false rhythms,

The formal construction.
He did not care even for the linguistic rules.
In other words, he did not juggle with truth.
On the contrary, things began to have their own simplicity,
Their own sweetness
But their own dangers as well.
He began to recite the text exactly as it is,
Truths exactly as they are;
Some poets are governors' pimps –
Or:
We live in times where lice eat poetry –
Or:
The poet is either a severed head or a sharp edge –
Or:
Let us swing this planet with our merciful
    and truthful hands.
At last, he says:
The poet must not be born sweet
But sweet and truthful.
At the same time he must be akin to Jesus
    and Disobedience
Must not be afraid even if he has fierce truth
Or eyes which praise fairness
And make our world naked.
He must not even fear
The gallows which await him
In the darkness.

In the second corner
On the left side of the injured heart,
Close to a white cloud,
The poet was killed,
Shot by an unknown hand
In a muddy ditch.

# CONTRIBUTORS

**Rear Admiral Eugene J. Carroll, Jr** is Deputy Director of the Center for Defense Information, an organization of retired senior military officers dedicated to monitoring Pentagon weapons systems, spending and policies. He was commissioned as an Ensign in 1945 and during his thirty-seven years of active service he was awarded the Defense Superior Service Medal, the Legion of Merit with three gold stars, the Bronze Star Medal with combat 'V' and gold star, the Air Medal with four gold stars and numerous campaign ribbons for service in World War II, Korea and Vietnam.

**Alexander Cockburn** is an Irish citizen, resident in the USA since 1973. He is a regular contributor to numerous publications including *The Nation* and the *Los Angeles Times*. His books include *Corruptions of Empire* and with Susanna Hecht, *The Fate of the Forest: Developers, Destroyers and Defenders of the Amazon*. A personal memoir, *Encounters with the Sphinx* is published in 1992.

**Andrew Cohen**, former editor of the *Yale Literary Magazine*, is a writer based at *The Nation*.

**Dr Fadia Faqir** was born in Amman in 1956. She gained her BA in English Literature, MA in Creative Writing, and doctorate in critical and creative writing at Jordan University, Lancaster University and East Anglia University respectively. Her first novel, *Nisanit*, was published by Penguin in 1988 and her second, *The Yarn-Spinner*, is forthcoming. Fadir Faqir is at present working on her third novel and teaching creative writing and Arabic language and literature at the University of Exeter.

**Faleh' Abd al Jabar** was born and educated in Baghdad. He left the country in 1978 and worked in Beirut and then Damascus as a journalist and researcher. He edited *An Nahj*, a bimonthly theoretical and political review. He now lives in London. He has written three books on fundamentalism, and other political and theoretical books.

**Haifaa Khalafallah** is an oil journalist who has worked in Kuwait. She is a winner of the International Association for Energy Economics Award for journalism in 1988 and a board member of Article 19, a London-based human-rights organization that monitors freedom of expression. She is currently studying for a doctorate degree in Middle East History at Georgetown University, Washington DC.

**Dr Lesley Morrison** was born in Scotland and now lives in London with her partner Joe, and their children, Rob and Iona. Initially a general practitioner, she is now a consultant in public health medicine and women's health in inner London and vice-chair of the Medical Campaign Against Nuclear Weapons, an organization dedicated to publicizing the links between disarmament, health, the environment and development.

**Roger Owen** is Director of the Middle East Centre, St Anthony's College, Oxford. His book, *State, Power and Politics in the Making of the Modern Middle East* will be published in early 1992.

**Grace Paley** is a short-story writer, author of three collections, and an active member of the American peace movement. She lives in Vermont.

**Edward Pearce**, Wednesday columnist of the *Guardian*, formerly (1979–87) parliamentary sketchwriter of the *Daily Telegraph*, has written five books, the most recent being a biography of the Prime Minister, *The Quiet Rise of John Major*, published in April 1991. He broadcasts regularly, notably in the Radio 4 series 'The Moral Maze', and has received the Granada Award for Columnist of the Year.

**Rear Admiral Gene R. La Rocque** is the Director of the Center for Defense Information, an organization of retired senior military officers dedicated to monitoring Pentagon weapons systems, spending and policies. In this capacity he has travelled to 105 countries to analyse the military situation in the world. He began his naval service in 1940 and spent thirty-one years in active duty including seven years in the Pentagon in strategic planning for the Joint Chiefs of Staff and the Chief of Naval Operations.

**Barbara Rogers** has worked as a consultant to the United Nations, UNDP and FAD and represented the World Federation of United Nations Assocations and other organizations for five years in the 1970s at the United Nations in New York, working on southern African and international development issues. Her first job was at the Foreign Office in London, where she worked on Namibia and UN aspects of South Africa. She now edits *Everywoman*, the woman's current affairs magazine.

**Sadiq al Saygh** is an Iraqi poet, journalist, calligrapher and literary critic. He left Iraq in 1978 and has lived in Beirut and Prague; he now lives in London. He has published two books of poetry in Arabic – *The Hymn of the Hippopotamus*, published in Baghdad in 1967, and *A Homeland for the Soul*, published in Beirut in 1981. He edited a quarterly review of work by Iraqi writers in exile, *Alternative*.

**Abbas Shiblak** was born in Haifa, but left Palestine with his family. He was educated in Egypt and Britain. After two and a half years as an academic in Algeria he came to London in 1975 and worked as a writer and journalist. For the past six years he has worked for the Arab League. He is the author of *The Lure of Zion: The Case of the Iraqi Jews*, published by Al Saqi books in 1987.

**John Vidal** edits the Environment Pages of the *Guardian*.